George Edwin Waring

Tyrol and the Skirt of the Alps

George Edwin Waring

Tyrol and the Skirt of the Alps

ISBN/EAN: 9783743435452

Printed in Europe, USA, Canada, Australia, Japan

Cover: Foto ©Andreas Hilbeck / pixelio.de

Manufactured and distributed by brebook publishing software (www.brebook.com)

George Edwin Waring

Tyrol and the Skirt of the Alps

TYROL

AND

THE SKIRT OF THE ALPS

By GEORGE E. WARING, Jr.

AUTHOR OF "A FARMER'S VACATION" ETC.

𝔍𝔩𝔩𝔲𝔰𝔱𝔯𝔞𝔱𝔢𝔡

NEW YORK

HARPER & BROTHERS, PUBLISHERS

FRANKLIN SQUARE

1880

TO

"JANE,"

THIS RECORD OF OUR WANDERINGS

Is Affectionately Inscribed

—IN ATONEMENT.

CONTENTS.

CHAPTER I.
UNDER THE WATZMANN 13

CHAPTER II.
PASS LUEG AND THE PINZGAU 24

CHAPTER III.
ZELLER-SEE AND ZILLER THAL 30

CHAPTER IV.
THOSE WHOM WE MET, AND THEIR WAYS 39

CHAPTER V.
THE CITY OF THE INN 44

CHAPTER VI.
THE PEOPLE AND THEIR LIFE 54

CHAPTER VII.
ACROSS THE BRENNER 59

CHAPTER VIII.
THE CITY OF THE BELLS 65

CHAPTER IX.
INTO THE GRÖDNER THAL 73

CHAPTER X.
A Day on the Seisser Alp 86

CHAPTER XI.
At the Foot of the Great Range 96

CHAPTER XII.
The Portals of the Dolomites 102

CHAPTER XIII.
Cortina D'Ampezzo 106

CHAPTER XIV.
The Ascent of Monte Tofana 116

CHAPTER XV.
To the Mesurina Alp 127

CHAPTER XVI.
From the Great Peaks to the Lagunes 131

CHAPTER XVII.
A Morning in the Streets of Venice 136

CHAPTER XVIII.
Circumlocution 142

CHAPTER XIX.
The Lakes 147

CHAPTER XX.
The Vaudois Valleys.—The Waldenses 160

CHAPTER XXI.
Into the Higher Valleys 166

ILLUSTRATIONS.

	PAGE		PAGE
Berg und Thal . . . . . *Frontispiece*		"Finger-hacking."—[From a Painting by Defregger]	57
The Watzmann, overlooking Berchtesgaden	15	Profile of the Brenner Railway	59
Peasant Girl	16	Parish Church, Botzen	62
Peasant	17	Meran, from the Kuchelberg	63
Entrance to the Königs-See	18	Schloss Tirol	69
Königs-See	19	Vineyard Watch	72
Lake in Salt-mine, Berchtesgaden	21	Alpen Rosen	74
Costume of the Salt-mine	22	A Village Street	75
Pass Lueg	25	St. Ulrich and the Lang Kofel	76
Schloss Fischhorn	28	Costume of Bride in the Grödner Thal	79
The Wilde Kaiser	31		
Hopfgarten	32	The Wood-carver	81
Farm-house	35	Tyrolese Costume, Val Sugana	82
Costumes of the Ziller Thal	37	A Mountain Porter	84
Edelweiss	44	The Lang Kofel, from the Seisser Alp	87
Maria Theresa Strasse, Innsbruck	45		
Goldenes Dach	46	Tyrolese Costume, Sarn Thal	88
King Arthur	47	Costume of the Dux Thal	91
Andreas Hofer	48	The Glacier of Marmolata	94
Philippine Welser, Countess of Tyrol	49	William Howitt	98
Terra-cotta Stove at Amras	51	Lienz, Puster Thal	100
Telfs	52	The Inn at Landro	103
"Wrestling."—[From a Painting by Defregger]	56	Schluderbach and the Croda Rossa	104
		Cortina and Monte Tofana	107

ILLUSTRATIONS.

	PAGE
Fresco on the outside of the Aquila Nera	109
Monte Antelao	112
Civita and Lake Alleghe	114
Cinque Torre and Nuvalau	117
Mesurina Lake and the Drei Zinnen	128
"The Women with their busy Distaffs"	133
Fireplace in Italian Inn at Fadalto	135
Balcony Marketing	138
At the Public Well. — A Morning Scene in Venice	140
Riva, from the Ponale Road	148
Tremosine, by Lake Garda	149
Lemon Garden, Lake Garda	150
Limone, Lake Garda	152
San Giovanni, Bellaggio, on Lake Como	154
Lecco	155
A Street in Bellaggio	157
From the Villa Serbelloni	158

TYROL,

AND

THE SKIRT OF THE ALPS.

CHAPTER I.

UNDER THE WATZMANN.

Our first look into the promised land was from the far crest of the Kapuzinerberg, where the balcony of the odd old bastion restaurant overlooks the broad and beautiful valley through which the Salzach pours its milky glacier torrent. Guarding its entrance stands the magnificent high-perched fortress of Salzburg. On either hand, coming close to the foreground, are the great gray peaks of the Gaisberg and Untersberg. Behind these, stretching away into the distance, rises crest after crest of the Salzburg Alps. The fear seemed reasonable that we had made a grave mistake in choosing this entrance to Tyrol, for we could not hope again to see such a combination of beauty and grandeur as this far-stretching, fertile plain and yonder snow-clad peaks. The fear abated before a day had passed, and it never recurred. Climbing down again to the low-lying town, we soon engaged an "Einspänner" to take us to Berchtesgaden.

One's first Einspänner is a memorable vehicle—queer-shaped, with a comfortable back seat, having its top thrown back in fair weather, and only a rudimentary front seat, from which the driver's feet fall directly upon the whiffletree. As the name indicates, it is drawn by one horse—harnessed, not between shafts as with us, but at the left side of a pole, with a cat-a-corner sort of traction by no means economical of power. Behind is a "magazin," in which smaller articles of baggage are locked, larger trunks being strapped upon its top. This is the universal one-horse vehicle of South-eastern Germany and Austria.

We trundled out of the town and over the country road at a pace which was to consume three hours in making the fourteen miles' distance. Half an hour out, at a foddering and beer-drinking station, we fell in with a "Zweispänner"—a comfortable two-horse landau—returning to the hotel for which we were destined. Our driver made a shrewd contract, by which we were to be carried the remaining long pull for one-half of our three-dollar fare. The change was in every way advantageous. Our road soon left the Salzach plain, and led up the wild and beautiful valley of the Alm; up hill and down dale, past chalets with stone-laden roofs, past the little fields of peasant farms, through groves of fir and white birch, and along the brink of the rapid white-watered river. Frequent hay for beast and frequent beer for man are constant incidents of Tyrol travel. Every few miles the team must be drawn up for baiting, and the blue-eyed Kellnerin brings beer as a matter of course; but the beer is good and the fare is cheap, and the hours thus dawdled away are by no means lost to one who comes fresh to all this unaccustomed beauty and interest. Time thus spent at way-side inns among costumed peasants here in the foot-hills of the great Alpine chain is time gained for the memories of all future years. We may have been three hours, or we may have been four hours, in going from Salzburg to Berchtesgaden; but should we live for fifty years, no time can dim the charming recollections of that drive.

Scattered along the road at very frequent intervals are the shrines and stations and crucifixes with which this whole land is disfigured. To the South German mind the tears of the Virgin and the cruel bodily suffering on the Cross seem to be the only effective emblems of Christianity. Generally absurd, often painful, and always coarse, these tokens are too frequent to excite reverence, and can have little other effect than to maintain the routine of the formal observances of the Church. The Madonna often wears hoops of enormous dimensions; she frequently weeps behind a painted handkerchief: in one instance, where she was of wood and of life size, she held the fresh-ironed linen with printed border of our own time. So little does the real character of the Crucifixion impress itself upon the popular mind, that it is by no means uncommon for the bleeding wound of the wooden Christ to be decked with flowers or ribbons on festival days. In one case a bunch of cat-tails was stuck between the knees. It is perhaps well for the tourist that these shrines occur so frequently, for their shock is weakened by familiarity, and one soon comes to pay little heed to them.

The valley of the Alm is too narrow, and offers too little chance for cultivation, for its agriculture to be more than the pettiest farming of a very poor and hard-worked people; but as it bends at last around the

THE WATZMANN, OVERLOOKING BERCHTESGADEN.

grand southern sweep of the Untersberg it widens out into broad and rich farms, overlooking which, occupying a high plateau, and itself overlooked by the gigantic Watzmann, lies the ideal Tyrolean village of Berchtesgaden.*

No doubt there are other places as charming, but none ever touched us quite so nearly as this. Its situation, its air, its evidence of having pleasure for its chief industry, and, above all, its picturesque people,

---

* This district is politically in Bavaria, but in all its characteristics it belongs to Austrian Tyrol, which it joins.

combine to make it quite a village by itself. It has to the stranger almost a suggestion of theatrical effect, greatly due to the marked costumes of the peasantry, who form so conspicuous an element of its population. Both men and women adhere to their national dress as firmly as though no Einspänner had ever brought a traveller from Salzburg to see them. On week-days it is sobered by the rust of long use, but it is still the same in its essential parts; on Sunday it is gay galore, and it is worth while to rise early and look out from a front window of the Hotel Watzmann as the people are gathering for early mass at the old church opposite.

PEASANT GIRL.

The accompanying illustrations give the dress of the whole peasant community, not touched up for artistic effect, but precisely as worn. The maidens depend much on color and on their broad silver necklaces with gaudy clasps, but the men's dress resembles that with which we are familiar only in coat and shirt. The breeches are of black leather, with green cord down the seams and green embroidery at the hip and knee; they reach only to the top of the knee, and are so loose that in the sitting posture half the thigh is exposed. No stockings are worn under the heavy hob-nailed shoes, but a very thick woollen stocking leg, often ornamented with green figures, covers the calf, the top being rolled down over the garter. For a length of about six inches at the knee the leg is quite bare, tanned, ruddy, and hirsute with life-long exposure in a climate of great winter severity. The hat varies but little from the form shown, and is decorated with feathers *at the back*—usually the half of a black cock's tail. This is the daily gear of these hardy mountaineers, and is the type of the national costume of the whole of North Tyrol. Nothing could be more artistic; but it must be a deeply planted artistic feeling which sustains the wearers in fierce winter weather. Grohmann (*Tyrol and the Tyrolese*) says that at a wedding rifle match, when the thermometer was at 4° Fahrenheit, he saw men come in their shirt sleeves and with bare knees from the hot dancing-room, and stand shooting for an hour, heedless of the cold.

Pleasant as Berchtesgaden is in itself, it owes its great attractiveness to the beautiful Königs-See, three miles away, at the end of a charming brook-side walk through a deep and thickly wooded valley. This lake is the pearl of Tyrolean waters. Statistically speaking, it is six miles long and a mile and a half wide. It is about two thousand feet above the level of the sea. Its inclosing mountains rise almost vertically from its shore, the snow-clad Watzmann to a height of nine thousand feet, and the others far above the line of vegetation. The deep water of the lake is emerald-green, cold, and clear.

It was on the stillest and sweetest of summer Sunday mornings that we first saw it. We shared a boat with a Viennese doctor and his pretty wife, and a kindly engineer of the salt-mines. For rowers we had a comely wiry-armed damsel and

PEASANT.

two tough-sinewed, bare-kneed, cock-feathered young men—one standing at his oar after the manner of a gondolier. They were a silent and steady-pulling crew, ready with information, but entirely unobtrusive. The boat-landing opens upon a beautiful fore-bay, shut in by high hills which form a bold foil for the gray and white mountains beyond them. This bay is soon crossed, and a turn to the right, around the steep rocks, brings the grand main stretch of the lake into view. On either hand rise the sheer mountain-sides, and straight

ENTRANCE TO THE KÖNIGS-SEE.

to the front the snow-clad Stuhlgebirge stands like a vast wall. Behind this chain is the head of the Schönfeldspitz, but little lower than the Watzmann, which dips its feet in the lake, and holds its snow-filled notch nearly a mile and a half overhead. It had rained heavily the day before, and the little rills which usually trickle down the mountain-sides were swollen to grand cascades, leaping from point to point of their quick descent.

We climbed into the deep ravine of the Kesselbach, where a mountain torrent has torn its rugged way and filled its path with huge blocks wrenched from the mountain. Again we landed to walk over to the pretty little Obersee, which lies in a lap of the hills at the far end of the lake; and again to eat the renowned Saibling, or lake trout, at St. Bartholomae—a toothsome *specialité* of the Königs-See—and to drink the perennial beer of the Vaterland. St. Bartholomae is a royal hunting château, which brings pence to the royal purse through the hunger and thirst of the visiting public. It is a grim old château, with a pious annex in the form of a gloomy little chapel, which invites many pilgrims on St. Bartholomew's Day. Its main hall is hung with rude portraits of giant Saibling taken in the lake during the past century, the honored name of its captor being given with each. These landings were not without interest—a large element of human interest, too, for the travellers to the Königs-See are various—but we always floated gladly back into the calm green deep lake, whence the enchanted setting of this enchanted mountain mirror seemed like a fairyland of the giants, reaching high overhead, and reflected far down in the still waters below.

KÖNIGS-SEE.

Each boat carries an old blunderbuss of a horse-pistol with which to awaken the echoes at the narrower part of the lake. These are quite remarkable. The pistol, being loaded with loose powder, gives only a thud of a report, which is instantly returned from the nearest shore by a loud cracking detonation, which is repeated with a muffled roar again and again, like the roll of receding thunder. I am quite at a loss to explain the single sharp first echo which was invariably heard.

It had been our privilege to go in a boat with three rowers for only five persons, and our four hours' trip—ever to remain unequalled—cost what the Schiffmeister regarded as an extra price—forty-four cents for each person.

For variety, and by way of indulgence to inexperienced feet, we took an Einspänner for our return home. The variety made it quite worth while, for the valley between Königs-See and Berchtesgaden is beautiful from every point of view, and the carriage-road takes quite a different course from that of the foot-path. We were driven by a young lout from a distant province, whose stock of information was exhausted when he had told us that a pretty modern villa near the road-side was owned by a Jew. We complimented the Jew upon his good taste and good fortune, and were quite content to accept the remaining miles of our road for their constant and changing beauty, without further detail. It mattered little who owned this or that; it sufficed that at every turn there opened a new picture.

The Watzmann was our constant attendant, and it seemed strange that while he looked so near, our whole journey kept him ever at the same angle. In the clear sky of that Sunday it was impossible to realize his distance, and only the eternal snow lodged between his two great bare peaks indicated his height. The guide-books give detailed instruction for reaching the summit of this mountain, and there are in Berchtesgaden stout-limbed and intelligent guides to carry one's kit and food and lead the way to the summit. But the mountain-climbing passion is an uncultivated one in my breast, and I am quite content to leave nature's great peaks all unbereft of the mystery and grandeur which they shed over those who wander wondering through the valleys at their feet. I do not intimate that familiarity with their crests would breed contempt, and I admire the enterprise and vigor which scorn the fatigue and suffering their ascent must entail; I only beg to be permitted for myself to confine my wanderings over this great and splendid world to fields which reward one with something different from the view of mountain-tops from mountain-top. This

LAKE IN SALT-MINE, BERCHTESGADEN.

may be a middle-aged weakness, and it may well be born of ignorance; but I gladly accept such familiarity with the mountains as one gains from the richly cultivated slopes and vales of Tyrol as quite sufficient.

On one of the days of our stay we explored, so far as the public is permitted to explore them, the great salt-works of Berchtesgaden, which are the property of the King of Bavaria. This is the show salt-mine of the world, and the act of visiting it was invested by old King Ludwig with the artistic and dramatic air of which he was so fond. There is little reason why the ten thousand who enter its galleries every year should not go in the every-day dress of the outer air; but party after party is daily clad in the garb of the miners, the ladies in a corresponding costume, as though the tour were attended with the dirt and discomfort of a coal-mine. The galleries are quite dry—so dry that where timber is used for supporting the roof it needs to be renewed only once in a century. The deposit is in the heart of a high hill. There are five gangways, one above the other. Visitors are taken in at the entrance of the lowest one, and only to the worked-out galleries of the second, but this suffices to give a good idea of the methods. The hill is entered for a distance of more than a mile, part of the way up a stairway of more than one hundred steps, and then on and on into the very bowels of the mountain. Salt exists in a very pure state to an unknown height above, and a shaft sunk one hundred and fifty metres below the lowest excavation fails to find its bottom.

The workings are of two sorts, the quarrying of rock-salt for cattle (four thousand tons per annum), and the extraction and transportation of pure salt, in solution in water, which is let in fresh from the hills above, left from four to six weeks to become impregnated, then drawn to a lower reservoir, whence it is pumped to Feisterleite, seven hundred feet higher on the mountain-side. Thence it flows through pipes to Ilsang, about four miles distant, where it is again lifted, this time twelve hundred feet, to the top of the mountain. From this point it flows through pipes, always on a descending grade, to Reichenhall, twenty miles distant. Here it is evaporated, the crystallized salt being ground for table use (from twenty-five to thirty thousand tons per annum). The average daily flow is over two thousand hectoliters. The pump by which this is raised is worked by a water-engine of brass (six-inch cylinder), constructed precisely like a steam-engine, and propelled by a column of water three hundred and seventy-four feet high. One hundred pounds of fresh water dissolves about twenty-seven pounds of salt, so that, in view of the abundant water-power, this system of transportation is most economical.

COSTUME OF THE SALT-MINE.

The large pools in the mine in which the salt is dissolved are most interesting. One which is no longer used is encircled with several hundred miner's lamps, which only make its darkness visible. Visitors are ferried over this pool in boats, and landed opposite an illuminated transparent block of salt inscribed with the miner's greeting, "Glück auf." The descent from here is by a steep slide over polished wooden rails, pitching at a sharp angle into the great pit where rock-salt was formerly quarried. A guide goes first in the line, and regulates the speed by a rope slipping under his arm. The visitors, sitting on the rails, make a close-packed train behind him. The exploration of the work completed, we are mounted, men and women together, astride the elevated cushion of a little car which runs at great speed down the descending track through the mile-long gallery, and out into the broad daylight and the heated open air. For those who care to perpetuate their absurdity, a photographer has set up his atelier hard by.

However short one's stay, Berchtesgaden must be quitted with regret, and in our case at least there came the feeling, repeated at so many places, that we should some day return here for a longer stay and a closer familiarity with its varied interests. We were as yet only at the threshold of Tyrol, and with at best time for only a sketchy run among its mountains and valleys.

CHAPTER II.

PASS LUEG AND THE PINZGAU.

WE departed, again in an Einspänner, with a driver who became friendly and instructive after his sharp bargain had once been driven. Our drive to Hallein did not differ greatly from that from Salzburg, save that at one of our halting-places we saw, perhaps for once and all, and only through a telescope at that, the agile chamois feeding quietly on the very face, as it seemed to us, of the perpendicular Untersberg. Hallein is a dull and dingy old town on the Gisela railway, by which we made the half hour's run to Golling.

From Golling the glory has all departed. In the good old post-coach days it had much renown as a chief starting-point of the wild and beautiful ways into Eastern Tyrol. It is a long, straight Alpine village on the mountain-side. Our windows commanded nearly the whole street, with its curious people and its unfamiliar customs. Where mountain brooks and springs are plenty the rain-fall is not caught and stored as with us. It rained hard the whole night through, and the long eave-troughs, reaching far beyond the wide overhanging roofs, poured their torrents into the roadway from a height of three or four stories, until it seemed as though the town itself must be washed into the valley.

I am fond of the Landsleute of German villages, and the country people who congregate of an evening in the beer-room of every Gasthaus have far more interest for me than their betters who travel, and who fill the guests' eating-room with bad tobacco-smoke. I sat at table with half a dozen of the wiseacres of the village, who were in warm discussion with a wandering Handwerker as to the propriety of the investment by the Golling community of three thousand gulden in making a better pathway into the renowned Oefen, a marvellous chasm in the

PASS LUEG.

mountain, through which the whole Salzach pours its flood. No city ever discussed the improvement of its harbor with more heated animation than was brought out by the two-sided question of spending $1500 on a local betterment, which, it was argued, would restore to Golling the cloud of visitors that the railway had diverted.

My next neighbor was a tall, raw-boned, grimy-faced, cheerful shoemaker of the village, who soon made known the fact that he was Johann Kain, a licensed mountain guide (Bergführer) of the province. He produced from a wallet at his belt the book containing his authority, the established tariff of charges, the obligations of the Bergführer, the penalties for his misconduct, and the signatures and commendatory remarks of his many patrons for long years past. As Baedeker tells us, one clearly needs no guide for the plain path over the Oefen and along the high-road through Pass Lueg to Sulzau; but a few hours with an original character like Kain would be well worth his fee of less than a dollar, and I was glad to engage him for the next day. The trip was the more interesting for his company, and it must be a marvellous two hours' walk under any circumstances.

The Oefen by far outmatches all other mountain gorges of which I have knowledge. The Salzach is really a great mountain river, fed by far-away glaciers and countless hill-side brooks. It drains the whole northern slope of the Alpine range from beyond the Grosser Venediger on the west to far east of Bad Gastein. During the preceding week unwonted rains had swollen every rill to a torrent, and the river itself was a boiling, rushing flood of turbid waters. It has torn its way through the high granite barrier, and mighty rocks from its higher cliffs have fallen across its chasm, forming natural bridges over the torrent, which are covered with grass and trees. Here and there, through great clefts, the river is to be seen surging far below with a deafening roar.

The descent from the heights of the Oefen strikes the highway at the entrance of Pass Lueg opposite the curious Croaten Loch—a strongly fortified and almost inaccessible cleft in the vertical mountain-side, large enough for a garrison of five hundred men, and an impregnable position until artillery was brought to bear upon the splintering rock which forms its roof. It was held by the Croatians in

SCHLOSS FISCHHORN.

1742, and in the patriotic war of 1809 it played an important part. For modern warfare it has no value, and is only a relic of the past; but Pass Lueg itself, six miles long, and often only wide enough for the river and the road, is an easily defensible pass, and the only practicable opening through the mountain east of the valley of the Inn. The Gisela railway passes its narrowest part by a tunnel. At the east the pass is dominated by the Tannengebirge, nearly eight thousand feet high. During the whole walk to Sulzau my old guide talked of the hills and valleys and passes within walking distance of Golling, which to him constitute the whole world, and beyond which he has never set his sturdy foot.

Having taken places in the observation car at the rear end of the train—a car with an open gallery looking to the rear and sides—we made a most memorable journey up the steep Salzach Valley and into the Pinzgau. At Werfen the road, leaving the narrow gorge, passes under the shadow of the high-perched fortress of Höhe Werfen, which is not unlike the one which at Salzburg guards its northern entrance. A writer cannot, without laying himself open to the charge of extravagance, repeat so often as the description of such a journey demands the superlative expressions which alone are adequate. The reader's highest imagination will surely not overpass the grand and beautiful reality.

A little further on we stop at Lend, the station for the renowned —Tyroleans think overrenowned—Wildbad Gastein; and as evening closes in, always looking back over the same succession of mountains, and always beside the tumbling stream, we round Schloss Fischhorn— Prince Liechtenstein's beautifully restored castle—commanding the Upper and Lower Pinzgau, the valley of the Zeller-See, and the Fusch Thal.

CHAPTER III.

ZELLER-SEE AND ZILLER THAL.

The Zeller-See differs from the Königs-See as much as one mountain lake can differ from another. At the first view it is disappointing, but a short stay at its bordering village of Zell restores all of its well-reputed glory. Its shores are everywhere low, and its surrounding mountains are distant; but as seen from the middle of the lake, their grand forms, and their bare crests, or snow-clad peaks under the ever-changing light and shadow of a cloud-filled sky, inclosing a vast and fertile basin, make a perfect combination of Tyrolean beauty. At the north, beyond the plain of Saalfelden, rises the rugged wall behind which lies the south-eastern projection of Bavarian Tyrol. Far away to the south, peering above the high green hill-tops, and hiding from sight the glacier crest of the Gross Glockner, is the snow-covered Kitzsteinhorn.

In a certain sense Zell has been spoiled by the railway. It is full of tourists, and its lake is always busy with pleasure-boats; but we have nowhere found more simplicity and quaintness than in the peasant's house where we were billeted, the hotels being overfull. The roaming visitors have made very little impression upon the native population. Outside the modern hotels a kreutzer counts for as much as ever, and the cheerful "Guten Tag" of all whom we meet in the streets is as frank as in the remotest valley. Our handmaiden, Teresa, was as amazed at our desiring more than a pint of water for our ablutions as though she had never seen a traveller before. She brought, quite cheerfully, a huge bread-bowl in place of the pudding-dishes we had found inconveniently small, and a third carafe of water. She did this with so much the air of having performed her whole duty that we were fain to restrict our needs to the insufficient supply. So far was she from expecting a gratuity for her prompt attendance that she blushingly added to our bill a charge of six cents for shoe-cleaning. Our large room, inclosed in thick stone walls, with iron-barred windows and heavy oaken door, was as safe as a fortress. One corner was occupied with a huge green glazed earthen-ware stove, set on a high stone foundation. The beds were good, the linen was clean, and the furniture included two cabinets—one filled with Christmas-tree decorations, and the other with Schützenfest prizes won by our host in the sharp-shooting days of his youth. Gaudy religious prints

THE WILDE KAISER.

adorned the walls, and comfortable and well-kept furniture made up the outfit of this "best chamber," for the use of which, with attendance, we were charged forty cents per day.

The boats of the Zeller-See are different from any that we have elsewhere seen. They are long, flat-bottomed craft, rising high at stem and stern, with comfortable high-backed seats amidships. They are propelled, like a gondola, with a single oar near the stern, where the oarsman stands at his work, facing forward. The oar has a most curious spoon-shaped blade, about two feet long and eight inches wide. It is considerably curved in the direction of its length, and slightly

HOPFGARTEN.

hollowed laterally. Its *convex* surface is its propelling surface. The rowlock is a foot high above the gunwale, and has an ingeniously contrived universal joint of iron. The end of the oar, about opposite the rower's breast, has a cross-handle. This is held in the left hand, and is used for giving the lateral movement needed to preserve the straight course in rowing at one side of the boat. The right hand is held lower down the stem. At first sight this struck me as the most outlandish and absurd paddle I had ever seen. Watching it at work, it seemed one of the best. During the greater part of the stroke its bearing against the water is at a right angle with the boat's course, and as it leaves the water the downward-turning blade seems to follow the exact curve needed to bring it out without splash and without resistance. So far as I could analyze its positions, it was doing effective work from the time the blade touched the water until it had entirely left it, and this can be said of no other oar that I have seen. These boats have a very holiday look, their sides and the broad oar blades being painted with corresponding figures and colors, usually diamonds of blue or red on white. The effect is complete when the boat is freighted with girls in light dresses, and carrying the blue or red parasols which here prevail, and is rowed by a costumed peasant.

We were fortunate in hearing the Tyrolean zither played by an accomplished master at a concert given during our stay at Zell. The capabilities of this instrument are far greater than would be supposed. In principle it is like a combination of the guitar and the harp.

The route from Zell to Wörgl on the Inn is best made by rail, the open observation car giving a view usually better than that from the lower-lying and frequently shaded highway. It is rich from end to end with grand mountain scenery, culminating in the great rugged masses of the Wilde Kaiser, and then toning down to the more rounded forms, the fertile slopes, and the placid valley where lies the Arcadian village of Hopfgarten.

As a convenient point from which to visit the Ziller Thal, we put up at the beautifully placed Gasthaus on the hill above Jenbach—a modern Swiss house, with a chalet gallery in front of our windows commanding a long stretch of the Inn Valley, its enclosing mountains, and the high snow peaks beyond Innsbruck.

The Ziller Thal is the most renowned, and I am ready to believe one of the most beautiful, of the pastoral valleys of Tyrol. It is purely pastoral, its two considerable towns having no industry not connected with agriculture, and its steep hill-sides being bright with farms and pasture alps to their summits. Rich woodlands occupy the rougher and steeper slopes and its deep-cut side valleys, which are noisy with tumbling water. Even more than other Tyrolese, the people of the Ziller Thal have always been given to seeking their fortunes through itinerant trade and minstrelsy. The money thus gained and the extreme fertility of the land have given them great prosperity. Farmers own their own farms, and there is an air of comfort and cheerfulness about their homes—notably a great profusion of flowers in the rich dark wood galleries of the chalets—which we do not see equalled among many more obviously wealthy people. Frugality and industry seem to go hand-in-hand with cheerfulness and activity. Among the older of both sexes there is much goitre, and the evidence of a hard-worked life; but the young girls especially are remarkably well-looking. On the whole, the Ziller Thal presents as favorable an example of a happy agricultural community as can be met with.

Zell, the capital of the upper valley, had been visited a week before our arrival with a devastating flood, the equal of which had not been known for centuries, and had suffered enormous damage. The water had risen in a single night higher than the tops of the door-ways; the church-yard in the centre of the town had been submerged; whirlpools had eaten great holes in the roadways; every bridge on the river had been swept away; and thousands of acres of the valley lands had been covered with slime, from which the water had even yet not entirely receded. Such a calamity befalling a less prosperous people would be well-nigh fatal; but here the loss can be borne without suffering, and the ultimate effect upon the valley lands will be beneficial, the detritus from the granite mountain-sides being of great fertilizing value. It must be some years before the beauty of the landscape is restored.

We found at Fügen a capital example of the Tyrolean "Wirth" in Samuel Margreiter, who keeps the Gasthaus zum Stern. Both he and his wife were members of Ludwig Rainer's company of Tyrolese musicians, and in their travels they have acquired a good knowledge of English. He is a handsome, hearty, cordial fellow, and a man of substance, to whom the traveller may be cordially commended. His musical specialty is the Hölzener-Gelächner (laughing-wood), known to us as the Zillerphone. It is made of sticks of fir-wood of different lengths, properly tuned by hollowing out their lower sides, loosely strung together, and resting on thin withes of straw. They are rung with little hard-wood mallets. Margreiter boasts that he taught the use of the instrument to the Princess of Wales and Princess Louise.

FARM-HOUSE.

He tells us that the costume of the valley in its full development is only to be seen on *fêtes*, as at rifle matches and weddings. To our foreign eyes marked traces of it were to be seen on every hand. The women almost universally, young and old, wear broad-brimmed, small-crowned, black felt hats, with thick gold or silver tassels lying on the front part of the brim; and the singular custom, not much noticed elsewhere, of carrying a carnation or other bright flower over the ear, prevails quite generally.

In the towns Zell and Fügen, and occasionally along the main road, the houses are large stuccoed stone structures, with projecting roofs and galleries, the stucco whitened and the wood-work sometimes painted. The detached farm-houses differ from those generally seen in other parts of the country in being almost invariably unpainted, their rich mellow-toned wooden upper stories and gables and their gray stone-laden roofs harmonizing perfectly with the landscape. Their mason-work, if colored at all, is either gray or buff. Rude frescoes of the Madonna or the Crucifixion are very common on the outer walls. The combination of house and stable under the same roof is in strong contrast to our customs; but the living-rooms of these houses are tidy and comfortable, and often more home-like and inviting than average agricultural interiors of our native land. There is a complete separation, by stone partition walls, between the house and its belongings. The main entrance and the rooms leading off from it are a sort of crypt with vaulted arches supporting the stone floor of the main story, where are the chief living-rooms. Under the roof are garrets, store-rooms, and bedrooms. Each floor opens on to its narrow gallery, and these are far overshadowed by the wide projecting roof, the ridgepole of which is longer than the lower edges, so that the top of the gable reaches forward considerably beyond the lower line of the eaves. Added to this forward pitch of the gable end, there is often a decided "batter" or buttress-like spread of the stone-built part of the house. Even those lines which are intended to be vertical or horizontal have had only the inadequate guide of the country carpenter's eye, so that parallel lines and right angles do not exist. The whole structure is a sort of free-hand drawing, which agrees charmingly with the combination of rounded and rugged forms that makes the whole landscape.

Tucked away in grassy nooks far up among the clouds, accessible only by the hardest climbing, are the little chalets of the Senners, or cow-herds, who pass the summer months in butter and cheese making, and who, especially when of the female sex, furnish the material for much of the romance and poetry of Tyrolean literature. This is the native home of the Jodel, the clear, penetrating language by which alone these widely separated and hard-worked hermits are able to greet each other across the valleys and noisy gorges, and by which at the end of the week the lusty youth of the valleys proclaim their coming to their mountain maidens.

ZELLER-SEE AND ZILLER THAL.   37

Probably no purely rural expedition would give more curious instruction, and surely none would be attended with more picturesque and romantic accompaniment, than a thorough exploration of the fertile slopes and the rugged high alps of the Ziller Thal.

COSTUMES OF THE ZILLER THAL.

We had another chief motive for halting at Jenbach in an intention to visit the Aachen-See, which lies eleven hundred feet up in the mountains, over seven miles of rough road. The descriptions, the photographs, and the reports of returning visitors indicated that while it is well worthy of a visit, and while its introduction would be necessary into any complete picture of Tyrolean travel, it did not so much differ from what we had already seen that we need face a steady and persistent rain for the sake of it.

Then, too, we had been long enough in the country for the impression of the great cities of the world to have faded, and we had little by little accepted the local estimate of the great metropolis of Tyrol, the chief centre of its civilization and the great source of its artificial supplies. We cherished, also, a charming recollection of a single autumn evening passed in its mountain-guarded streets, and of the twilight vesper service in the Hofkirche among the bronze shades of Maximilian and his chosen attendants. Better a day of what Innsbruck has to offer than the Aachen-See under low clouds and drizzling rain.

Our route lay up the valley of the Inn — a fast-flowing stream which drains the north slope of the Alps from the head waters of the Salzach to the borders of Switzerland — a stream which has torn its broad way through the mountains, and has filled its valley with rich deposit. As seen from the hill-tops, it is a thread of a river winding through a wide and fruitful valley which rises gently to the feet of its enclosing walls. Here, as everywhere, agriculture is the life and soul of the industry, and a constant succession of broad fields of Indian-corn filled it with the air of luxuriance which this alone of northern crops can give. The valley is rich in shade and fruit trees, its higher slopes are beautifully wooded, and its smiling modern houses and dull old castles indicate the age and persistence of its prosperity.

CHAPTER IV.

THOSE WHOM WE MET, AND THEIR WAYS.

WE were the more struck with the cheapness and rusticity of our entertainment, because many who have written in these later years complain that Tyrol, filled with travellers from all countries, has been bereft, even in its remotest hamlets, of all its original simplicity: that bumptious Americans and Englishmen have driven the modest Kellnerin from the dining-room, and substituted the *garçon* of the Swiss hotels. So far as I can judge, this is not at all the case. Even in much-frequented Gasthäusern the waiting is almost universally done by the Oberkellnerin and her maidens, the old customs of kitchen and table are still adhered to, and the prices charged preclude the idea of an advance having been made.

The Hotel Krone, on the bank of the lake at Zell, is entirely modern, sufficiently good and sufficiently costly; its men-waiters wear dress-coats, and it has nothing in common with the native Gasthaus. But one need not lodge at the Krone—we did not, because we could not—and it has had no more influence over the customs of the village, nor even over those of the old Gasthaus Krone, of which it is an outgrowth, than if it were twenty miles away. On the whole, I think it has been too much the custom to decry "tourists."

Of course it is pleasanter to have a whole compartment to yourself on the railway, and to find hotel servants devoted to you only. If you are of a certain constitution, it is gratifying to feel that you alone of all the enlightened world have been permitted to gaze upon this water-fall, to drink beer at this remote Gasthaus, or to tread this mountain path. But neither railway carriages, nor hotels, nor waterfalls, nor beer, nor mountain paths, were created only for us. No word so lacks a definition as that one over whose illustration Thackcray expended a volume without yet clearly fixing its meaning. I have sometimes wondered whether the real snob may not be the ultimate development of that incipient feeling which the best of us must recognize among the emotions with which we greet a stranger coming to the vacant seat beside us. For my own justification, I am glad to believe that all mankind has this same instinctive distaste for encroachment. The remarkable feature of the case is that so many intelligent persons capable of enjoying travel to the fullest extent, and capable of communicating their enjoyment to others, should fail to see that the only field wherein to exercise their passion for original adventure is in those undeveloped wilds which are always open for their exploration.

The inhabited world — certainly the whole of Tyrol — is public ground. It has been a favorite field for travelling since travelling began. No one can say how much of its very essence it owes to its long communication with the outer world. Even the remotest valleys furnish their quota to that great army of Tyrolese peddlers and wandering minstrels which has for centuries overrun all Christendom, generally returning to end their days on their native hill-sides.

If external intercourse has "spoiled" this people, we surely have not to blame the occasional foreign sojourners among them. My own idea is that they are and will remain less affected by the encroachments of travel than most other peoples. The returning wanderer, bringing back no foreign ways, resumes at once his Tyrolean life and character. Quite naturally, about the large towns and much-frequented health resorts, costumes and local customs recede somewhat to the background; but in Tyrol it is still a very near background. In the busiest street of Innsbruck, and about the Kursaal at Meran, broad necklaces, bright colors, bare knees, and hat feathers are by no means exceptional. In the side streets of either town there is no more suggestion of any foreign influence than there was before railroads had been invented.

While pleading in behalf of the inevitable, I must say a word, too, in defence of the much-abused railway; even more, I confess my profound obligation to it. But for its kind intervention I should pass this calm and peaceful Sunday morning not here, writing this record under the vine-clad hills and beside a swift-running Tyrol river; I should probably be writing long-neglected letters at Newport—if, indeed, without the railroad's help I had ever emigrated even so far as that from my native Connecticut village. The railways of Tyrol pass through most charming scenery, and the device has yet to be invented which is to equal in its value to the pleasure-seeker the "Breakwagen" and observation car of the Gisela road.

Having once taught ourselves not to detest our fellow-travellers, we have come to regard them with great interest. They are almost exclusively Germans, and most largely from the very large middle class—probably persons in small business and small professions who have economized throughout the year for the sake of a frugal excursion in summer. It is not clear that they interest us more than we interest them, but they have certain characteristics which to the American observer are very marked.

I have long been familiar, in literature and in fact, with the prandial methods of Continental Europeans, but each new experience develops new possibilities of the art. As a study of the adaptation of the means to the end, no field of investigation is richer. Photography has still one achievement to make in securing an unsuspected instantaneous view of the *table-d'hôte* of a German hotel. The processes beggar description.

I make no question that there is a class of European society which partakes of its food in a manner according with our conventions, but it sends very rare representatives over any road which we have travelled. Among the coarser and uncultured of every society we expect little deference to the requirements of delicacy. But to see a pretty, dainty, tastefully dressed, sweet-looking young woman bearing both elbows hard on the table, stabbing her meat by a backhanded blow with a fork, twisting her wrist and lowering her mouth to a convenient pitching distance, with the alternate by-play of a knife-blade charged with softer viands, produces a shock which no familiarity can soften. Only yesterday I saw a mild-eyed bride thus engaged, with the occasional interpolation of a pickled onion by her fond and admiring husband's deft harpoon. The effect was heightened by her vigorous quaffing of a full liter of beer during the meal. Taking this example—by no means an isolated one—from the more refined sex and class as a standard, I may safely leave to the reader's imagination the athletic exercises in a like direction of stalwart, hungry, and ambidextrous men. Vale!

This, however, by the way. I speak of it only as a noticeable custom of the people. It is a custom only; it is not rooted in any defect of character. Accepted in a kindly spirit, our German fellow-travellers seem amiable, happy, kindly, affectionate — and too often noisy. They evince far more pleasure in their travel than do the rarer English and the very exceptional Americans who cross our path. The appreciation of fine scenery which draws the English to this land is not a demonstrative appreciation. As a rule they go sedately, silently, and most respectably on, without touching with even the hem of their garments the real essence of the people among whom they wander. The Americans are more varied and individual, but by no means always more admirable. As an example: we encountered on the Brenner railway two of our compatriots, clearly an Eastern merchant and his new wife, pretty and well dressed. Their language and enunciation indicated fair education, and their silence suggested proper breeding. Their occasional speech was marvellous to hear. The man's sole observation concerning Innsbruck was that he had "never had a better meal at a way-station." Through the most majestic parts of the valleys of the Sill and the Adige he slept soundly. Never a Schloss or Schlucht did they notice. She, justified in her opinion that she had a very pretty hand and rings, spent much time in drawing on and off her gloves. After doubling the great ox-bow at Gossensass, by which a descent of over five hundred feet is accomplished in a direct distance of a few hundred yards, she expressed her disapprobation of such a waste of travel. She did not see "why the engineer couldn't let us go straight on." Arrived at Brixen, she roused her drowsy lord with, "Oh, here's one of those queer things Maggie told us about!"

Without rising to look, he asked, "What is it?"

"Why! don't you remember? A priest"—pointing to a huge brown-frocked Franciscan friar, and giggling merrily.

All else that they said and did was equally appreciative, and one could readily imagine the satisfaction with which they would return to the more congenial surroundings and companionship of their native life, and assert their clear conviction that Continental travel offers little that need tempt an American to a second trial.

I have made this digression touching the people whom we meet, partly to show that the encountering of them is by no means an unmixed evil. No human soil is so barren as not to yield fruit of wayside entertainment. No nation and no class fails to produce its food for reflection.

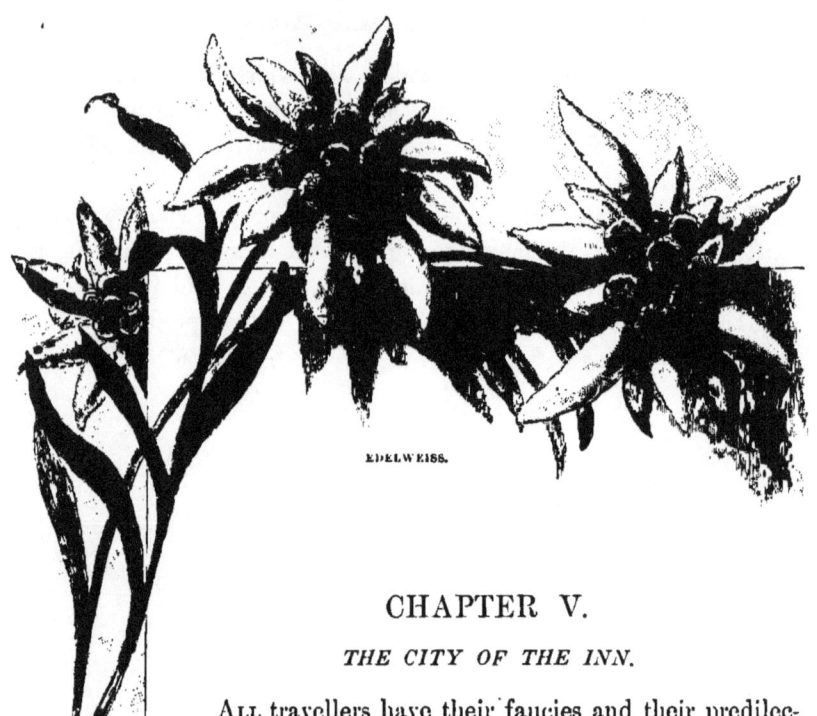

EDELWEISS.

EDELWEISS.

CHAPTER V.

THE CITY OF THE INN.

ALL travellers have their fancies and their predilections. I am by no means alone in giving the brisk little Innsbruck a high place among my own. Heine rung its praises fifty years ago: "Innsbruck ist eine unwohnliche, blöde Stadt." Another has called it a "pearl in Austria's beautiful crown of cities." It was the Emperor Maximilian's favorite town, and the beautiful Philippine Welser loved it hardly less than she graced it.

A single autumn twilight and starlight glimpse, years ago, impressed upon our own minds a picture of quaint and curious interest, of bright and cheerful beauty, and of grand and noble surroundings, which had lasted undimmed through the intervening time, and which is now only brightened and freshened and more deeply imprinted by familiarity with scenes which then were only suggested. In detail, there is not very much to describe, but the little that there is is most noteworthy. The *tout ensemble* is lively, bustling, cleanly, and handsome. Our windows look out upon the broad main thoroughfare of the town—a street of great width and finely built. In front of us stands a tall marble shaft-bearing the statue of St. Anna, its high base surmounted by life-sized figures. Far away to the left, over the tops of the houses and over the triumphal arch of the time of Maria Theresa, are the blue peaks bordering the Brenner Pass. To the right, rising like a vertical wall, as if from the very heart of the town, is the sturdy snow-streaked mountain, whence the wolves, as is told, used to look down into the streets and startle the citizens with their hungry howling. From the cab-stand below us the drivers of the odd little three-cornered Einspänners beckon us to drive. Yonder, above the dim arcades of the older town, beside the broad roof of the palace, rises the tower of that little court church which is more full of historic and artistic interest than many a great cathedral — a church whose broad nave is nearly filled with the superb sarcophagus of the great Emperor Maximilian I.

MARIA THERESA STRASSE, INNSBRUCK.

The chief of Innsbruck's street sights is the "Goldenes Dach:" a heavily gilded copper balcony roof, which Count Frederick of Tyrol— surnamed "of the empty pocket"—built against the front of his palace in 1500, at a cost of $70,000, as a substantial refutation of the popular taunt. The palace is long out of date, and the old quarter in which it stands is given over to the commoner walks of trade; but this beautiful balcony, with its gilded roof, still remains the richest monument of the city's streets. The large park and the shaded walk beside the swift-rolling Inn might well grace a larger and richer town; but these and all else that Innsbruck has to offer must give way before the attractions of Maximilian's tomb.

GOLDENES DACH.

Subsequent visits have served to define but not to materialize the unearthly impression remaining from the first one, made in the dusk of a warm November evening, when the gloom of the church was deepened by the solitary altar light and the faint glimmer of candles in a hidden chapel where vespers were being chanted. High up in the middle of the church the kneeling form of the robed monarch faces the altar. At the corners of the slab on which he rests are beautiful figures, and the sides and ends of the sarcophagus are panelled with twenty-four reliefs in marble, representing prominent events of his life. Most of these are by Alexander Colin (sixteenth century), and were said by Thorwaldsen to be the most perfect existing work of their class. The sarcophagus is enclosed by a light grille of the most graceful and delicate iron-work, richly gilded. Seen from the entrance of the church, this fine tracery is in harmony with the exquisite wood-carving of the first line of pews. At each side of the nave, between the large pillars, and at the ends of the altar steps, stand colossal bronze statues of the emperor's family, his chosen friends, and his most admired heroes—twenty-eight in number. Both the tomb and these surrounding figures were made in accordance with his own instructions, and in compliance with his last will. Aside from his relatives and family connections, the company includes Clovis, King of France, Rudolph of Hapsburg, Theodoric, King of the Ostrogoths, King Arthur of England, Godfrey de Bouillon, and Ferdinand of Aragon. Of these, the Theodoric and Arthur, by Peter Vischer, of Nuremberg, are of great artistic merit, the Arthur especially so. The others, by different artists, are often grotesque and curious; but as a company of guardian spirits about a great man's tomb they lend a dignity which no other device could compass. They certainly give an interest to this small church which distinguishes it in a very marked way from all others.

KING ARTHUR.

Without this tomb and its accessaries the church would still be memorable as being the burial-place of the great Tyrolean patriot, Andreas Hofer, who, rising from the position of a village innkeeper (always a position of distinction among Tyrolean peasants), became the leader in the uprising against the Bavarians. He was to Tyrol what Garibaldi has been to Italy. His house in the Passeier Thal is a chief historic centre of the country, and the rooms in which he slept during his campaigns possess a similar interest for the people to that of those in which Washington slept in his campaign through New England. His portrait in the museum at Innsbruck represents a sturdy Teutonic countryman, gorgeous with the embroidery and green and red of the costume of his valley. The engraving here given is after the miniature which is considered the most faithful likeness. Here, too, are tablets commemorating the death of Hofer's comrades, Haspinger and Speckbacher, and a fine modern monument to those who fell under their lead.

ANDREAS HOFER.

In a chapel adjoining the church, founded by Ferdinand II., Count of Tyrol, are his grave and that of his wife, Philippine Welser.

The central figure about which the interest of this region most gathers is that of this beautiful daughter of an Augsburg merchant, who made here her cherished home, whose virtues and gentle character no less than her beauty so fixed her memory in the hearts of the people, that she is as real a personage to them now as when she lived among them three hundred years ago, and who has rescued her worthy husband from the oblivion which, in much less than three centuries, so few escape.

PHILIPPINE WELSER, OF AUGSBURG, COUNTESS OF TYROL.

Their castle, Amras, stands on a superb hill an hour's drive from the town. The view from it reaches from the highlands of Bavaria to the lofty peaks of the Upper Inn, and stretches across the fertile maize-grown plain to the great snow-covered mountain back of Innsbruck. It is now the property of the Emperor of Austria, and the principal parts of its artistic collection, formed by Ferdinand, as well as the best portrait of its beautiful mistress, the original of the preceding cut, have been removed to the Imperial Museum at Vienna. It is still, however, rich in objects of great interest, having a fine collection of armor and arms, and the best of the furniture of Philippine's apartments. Among these are rare cabinets, organs, spinets, and writing-tables of the choicest workmanship, and of extravagant cost. In many of the rooms the fine old carved four-posters are still standing, and the countess's bedroom is still furnished as when she used it, including the cradle in which her babies were rocked. The collection of portraits is of great interest, among them one of Philippine Welser at fifty-two, still beautiful, and a late portrait of Maria Theresa in her widow's dress. Most of the rooms were heated with highly ornamented terra-cotta stoves. Even in these minor details the profuse expenditure, which is everywhere noticeable, is conspicuous. The whole castle is beautifully maintained, and one needs to be told, so rich is it still, for the time when it was occupied, that its chief treasures have been taken away.

It is not the least good thing about Innsbruck that its surroundings afford most charming walks and drives. We drove one afternoon up the zigzag course of the great Brenner highway, climbing always, but always gently, up the valley of the Sill, made more interesting now by the remarkable construction of the Brenner railway, whose cuttings and tunnels and arches and embankments, seen from the opposite heights, look like toy marvels of Lilliputian engineering. Such a combination of rich hill-side, wooded slope, deep gorge, rushing glacial river, rocky mountain top, and peaceful sunlit beauty is rarely seen. Closing the view before us, and rising like a barrier against the apparent trend of the valley, stands the great pointed peak of the Serlos.

Leaving the road and climbing a short, steep cart path, we come suddenly upon the deep and steep-sided Stubaier Thal, at whose head, lapping over the edge of a great mountain-top, hangs the eternal Stubaier Glacier. This is the very heart of the mountains — a valley scored deep among their highest peaks. The group by which it is surrounded carries no fewer than eighty glaciers, four of them of the first rank. No less than forty peaks to which its side valleys lead are close to the ten thousand-foot line of elevation. Other members of the Oetz Thal group, and other gorges draining their glacial floods away, help to make up this wildest centre of the Tyrolean Alps.

Our view into this valley of grandeur was from a sweet-smelling hay-field, where cheerful women and girls were raking the windrows,

TERRA-COTTA STOVE AT AMRAS.

where fragrant-breathed cows were drawing hay-wagons, and where sturdy men were busy loading the fresh-cured crop.

Far down in the valley, high up on its little alps, and clinging to its steeper acclivities, farm-houses and Sennerin's huts and peaceful

TELFS.

villages shelter a population to whom this mountain valley is the centre of the universe, who here toil and weep and love and die, all unconscious of the great world which lies beyond their almost impassable cliffs. The field where we sat belongs to the great mountain Gasthaus, where Andreas Hofer held his last head-quarters. It is a very large house, and its cheerful Kellnerin showed us all its mysteries: its clean bedrooms; its "Speise-Saal;" its quaint old wood-finished "Sitz," where the peasants gather for their evening beer; its milk-room, with brimming pans and well-scoured utensils; its stables for horses and cattle—all under the same huge roof; its ornamental garden, with a little fountain, and the saints and Madonnas frescoed on its outer walls.

It would be ungrateful to dismiss the subject of Innsbruck without referring to Mr. Franz Unterberger and his shop, which is a sort of travellers' head-quarters, stored with wood-carvings, Tyrolean knick-knacks, and the beautiful collection of photographs which his enterprising camera has brought from all quarters of the land. " Bild-hauing" (picture-hewing), or ornamental wood-carving, is nowhere more artistic than in this part of Tyrol, and Unterberger's exhibits at Philadelphia and at Paris gave evidence of the great excellence here attained. The relief carvings of Tyrolean character scenes are incomparably fine. To a stranger the best thing about the shop is Mr. Unterberger himself. He speaks English perfectly, and is a man of the quickest intelligence, and learned in Tyrolean matters. We found him always ready, without the least reference to his interest in us as customers, to give us the fullest information and advice.

The valley of the Inn above Innsbruck—the Oberinn Thal—lies out of the route of ordinary travel, the Brenner road striking off to the left and winding up the wild Sill Thal. The upper valley presents the same general character as that below the city, save that its mountains are drawn closer together, and its bed, rising higher and higher, comes nearer to their summits. It is essentially a part of this "Val Deliciosa," fertile, populous, busy, and cheerful. Telfs, one of its considerable villages, is a charming example of the larger valley centres. In its remoteness it promises to remain forever unconscious of the march of more modern improvement.

The summer heats of the Inn Thal are far greater and more persistent than would be supposed from its position on the northern slope of the Alps and its considerable elevation (Innsbruck is nearly two thousand feet above the sea). Its intervale for miles is almost exclusively occupied with broad fields of Indian-corn, giving it a home-like air to the American eye.

CHAPTER VI.

THE PEOPLE AND THEIR LIFE.

A GOOD idea of the characteristics of the country and the people of North Tyrol is given by Grohmann in his "Tyrol and the Tyrolese," from which one may gather information concerning the winter climate and occupations unknown to those who only make a holiday run through the country in the summer months. Mr. Grohmann is half Tyrolese himself, and seems to be as familiar with the hardy sports of the country as with those of England, where his other half belongs.

He describes vividly the terrible straits to which the frugal Tyrolese peasants are reduced by the deep and persistent snow, which entirely cuts off many of the valleys from communication with the outer world for months together. Mountain huts are sometimes entirely buried. He recounts the rescue of an aged couple who had been imprisoned for nine days, with only a goat and a few loaves of bread for their support. Chamois-hunting and the shooting of the blackcock, both confined to the higher and more remote mountain-tops, are sports involving the greatest fortitude and power of endurance, and are always attended with danger.

For a picture of Tyrolean life in the remoter valleys I know of nothing so striking and effective as a little story called *Geier - Wally*—nothing the reading of which so exactly anticipates the impressions which one's first trip produces.

The persistence with which humanity attaches itself to fertile land without regard to danger is illustrated elsewhere than here. The peasants on the slopes of Vesuvius push their cultivation and plant their homes in the very track of a possible lava stream, and, all the world over, facility for obtaining a livelihood blinds the cultivator to all risks. Grohmann says: "In the Wild-Schönau, North Tyrol, not a few of the houses are built on such steep slopes that a heavy chain has to be laid round the houses and fastened to some firm object—a large tree or bowlder of rock higher up.... In one village off the Puster Thal, and in two others off the Oberinn Thal, many of the villagers come to church with crampons on their feet, the terrible steep slopes on which their huts are built, somewhat like a swallow's nest on a wall, requiring this precautionary measure.... In Moos—a village not very far from the Brenner, having a population of eight hundred inhabitants—more than three hundred men and women have been killed since 1758 by falls from the incredibly steep slopes upon which the pasturages of this village are situated. So steep are they, in fact, that only goats, and even they not everywhere, can be trusted to graze on them, and the hay for the larger cattle has to be cut and gathered by the hand of man."

I have myself seen, in walking among the hills, little stores of hay piled against the upper side of protecting trees, where it had been brought in armfuls when cut and cured by the spike-shod hay-makers, who gather their little crops here and there on the steep grass-patches, almost at the limit of vegetation, pack it in nets or in sheets, and bring it on their shoulders down the steep and dangerous paths.

My earlier idea of an "alp" was that of a level plateau at the top of the lower mountains. Alps which are even nearly level are very rare, especially among the higher elevations. Generally they are so steep, so broken, and so inaccessible that one wonders how cattle are got to them, and how they can be trusted to graze over them. These alps are bounded by no fences, and it must be an anxious task for those who have the herds in charge to get them safely together at milking-time. Each animal wears its bell, not the hollow-sounding dull cow-bell with which we are familiar, but musical in tone, and heard for a much greater distance. The Alpine hut, and the Sennerin, or dairy-maid, who spends the whole summer in nearly solitary attention to her hard duties, are not altogether what one's imagination might depict. She is not the dairy-maid of poetry, nor is her temporary home filled only with the more ethereal pastoral associations. Yet these people, too, have a romantic and imaginative side to their lives, and are happy and wholesome and content.

The agriculture of North Tyrol, outside of the valley of the Inn, is mostly confined to very small operations. A few cattle, a few sheep, a little poultry, a few small fields, and a mountain pasture constitute the stock in trade on which the industrious and frugal pair bring up their family in comfort and decency, accumulate portions for

"WRESTLING."—[FROM A PAINTING BY DEFREGGER.]

their daughters, and lay aside a provision for their own old age. Labor-saving hardly exists. Everything is accomplished by unmitigated and unremitted toil. In youth and in early life the people are stalwart, active, and hearty; but old age comes very early, and at forty the vigor of manhood and womanhood is passed — the activity and vigor, but by no means the endurance: up to really old age even slight little women carry enormous loads in the baskets at their backs up and down steep rough hill-sides and mountain paths, where an untrained tourist must puff and toil to move his own unencumbered person.

It is not easy to see how in a country so broken as this, and where so many farms and even whole villages have no access to market except over mountain foot-paths, any system could be introduced which would lighten the labor of the people. On not one farm in fifty in the mountain valleys could the mowing-machine be used, and from at least one-half of the hay and grain fields the whole crop has to be carried away on the heads and shoulders of the people. Something might be gained by the introduction of a better race of cattle, but it is a question whether these too would not deteriorate under the constant exercise needed to pick up a living on these broken pastures.

The conditions of living are very much modified by the wandering propensity which is so common among the Tyrolese. As musicians, as peddlers, as cattle-dealers, and as mechanics, they travel over the wide world, bringing home a comfortable profit and a quickened intelligence.

"FINGER-HACKING."—[FROM A PAINTING BY DEFREGGER.]

The mental and moral characteristics of any people can of course be only very imperfectly measured by a casual traveller. The Tyrolese are represented as being extremely superstitious and priest-ridden, but no evidence of this was obvious to me. They are unquestionably honest and faithful, and universally temperate. Probably every man, woman, and child in Tyrol drinks beer and wine as constantly and as freely as we drink water; but during all of my journeyings in all parts of the country I have not seen a single person either drunk or under any considerable influence of drink. There are, too, very slight evidences of poverty, and beggars are rare. Among themselves, especially at the Gasthäusern in the evening, the younger men are noisy and uproarious, and much given to bad music and harsh play. Some of their games are rough to brutality, and it is not long since the use of the knife was a constant accompaniment of their quarrels.

Wrestling and "finger-hacking" (hooking the middle fingers and twisting for the mastery, even at the risk of the joint) are still common, and are watched by comrades with the same interest which attaches to a cock-fight or a dog-fight in England. Among a people the conditions of whose life make physical endurance a cardinal virtue, these trials of strength and of the ability to endure pain are regarded as tests of manliness, and even the women who witness them applaud their most brutal manifestations.

CHAPTER VII.

ACROSS THE BRENNER.

There are few railways more interesting to a traveller familiar with the construction of public works than that which crosses the Brenner Pass from Innsbruck to Botzen. It is nearly eighty miles long, and was built in four years. The natural difficulties were even greater than those of the Semmering, or of the Apennine road from Pistoja to Bologna.

Within a distance of little more than twenty miles it makes an ascent of 2500 feet, with a nearly uniform gradient of one in forty. Its escarpments and embankments are prodigious, and their protection

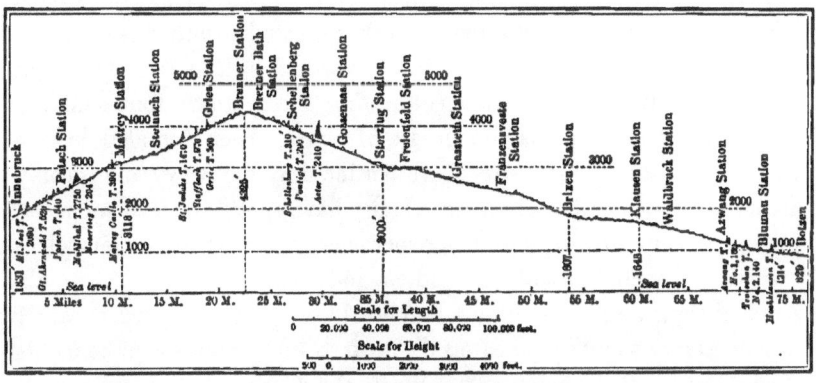

PROFILE OF THE BRENNER RAILWAY.

against the wash of the mountain-side is admirably provided for. At one point, where the banks of the Sill offered only an insecure foundation for the abutments of a bridge, the river itself was turned by a tunnel through the rock, the old bed being crossed on an embankment. The road passes through twenty-two tunnels, the longest of them 2750 feet. Several of these tunnels are built on considerable curves, and of one near Gossensass both of the mouths are in sight from the car windows at the same time. The scenery traversed throughout the whole distance is of the wildest and most romantic character; and as the road follows the course of the old highway between Germany and Italy, it is full of historic interest, from the repeated and stoutly contested struggles for its possession from the time of the Romans down to that of Andreas Hofer. Old castles and monasteries, some in ruins, some still occupied by private families, some turned to Stadthauses and some to breweries, give that marked difference which always exists between European scenery and our own. After crossing the Brenner Pass the course of the road strikes the valley of a little brook which gathers re-enforcements as it goes, and becomes a roaring river—the Eisach—long before it falls into the Adige at Botzen.

Botzen lies 3500 feet below the summit of the pass, deep down between the red porphyry cliffs by which its plain is bordered, and in the luxuriant climate of North Italy. The hill-sides and the valley are covered with abundant vines, grown on thickly covered sloping trellises; and, by slow-turning wheels of Egyptian device, the Eisach lifts up its water to irrigate the grass that grows beneath them.

As Innsbruck is the metropolis of North Tyrol, so is Botzen that of South Tyrol. But what a suffocating, close, stuffy, foul-smelling metropolis it is! It has the credit of having been founded by the Romans, and its business streets are bordered by the heavy and gloomy arcades common to hot climates. Many have spoken of it as a charming town; but in our repeated experiences we have found ourselves assailed by such indescribable odors and oppressed by such an absence of light and cheerfulness that we have come to regard it rather as a necessary stopping-place on the road to other points. Whence its smells come,—its street smells, I mean, the source of its house smells is too obvious to be doubted,—I have never been able to discover; for Botzen is essentially a city of clean streets. It is well supplied with fountains of clear water, and the turbid tide of the Adige sends a copious and rapid flow through all its streets. This latter runs through covered gutters with openings at frequent intervals, where women kneel over their wash-boards as at a brook-side.

It was a stifling hot night when we arrived, and we supped in the open air in front of a restaurant. The broad sidewalk was already filled with guests, and our table was set out in the open roadway, where friendly dogs assisted at our meal, and made themselves and us much at home. The fare was unusually good, and I had the curiosity to make a memorandum of our *menu* and of our bill, which is as follows (for two persons):

English fillet of beef, with egg	0.430
Potatoes, *sautées*	0.043
Macaroni à l'Italienne	0.043
Salad, with cheese	0.156
Omelette aux confitures	0.112
Tyrol red wine (one bottle)	0.120
One cup of coffee with milk	0.016
One cup of black coffee	0.008
One cigar	0.030
Fee to waiter	0.125

Making a total of one dollar, five cents, and three mills.

Botzen has a church of somewhat celebrated beauty, and the piazza commands a glorious view of the high-perched Rosengarten, one of the most characteristic groups of the whole dolomite formation, more completely a collection of grand "pinnacles" than any other that we have seen. The view of this followed us well out on the road toward Meran, through the broad and fertile Adige Valley, luxuriant with fig-trees and vines, with olives, tall cypresses, and all the characteristic vegetation of the South, walled in and sheltered on both sides by grand porphyry mountains, high up on whose slopes the hardy cultivators of its rich soil have planted their farm-houses and their hamlets. We were still in Tyrol, near the castle, indeed, which gave its name to the country, but in the richest valleys of Lombardy and Venetia we could not have been surrounded by a landscape of more thoroughly Southern aspect.

The nobles and the monks of the olden time knew well how to select the most beautiful and commanding sites for their habitations, and the high hill-sides of the Adige Valley are as rich as the banks of the Rhine with the ruins of their castles and their monasteries.

PARISH CHURCH, BOTZEN.

At Terlan, an hour's drive from Botzen, the village church has a conspicuous leaning tower, said to have been built by the architect of the tower of Pisa, who is claimed by the Tyrolese as a countryman. If the tower of Pisa is no more successful in its architectural effect than the tower of Terlan, it is a shabby builder's trick, without beauty and without special interest. The Terlan tower is a very large one, and is inclined at an awkward and uncomfortable angle; but its centre of gravity falls well within its base, and no especial skill was needed in its construction. The tradition of the neighborhood says that it was built erect, and has taken its inclination from a settlement of the foundation, which rests in the alluvial deposit of the valley, and is often deeply submerged by the floods of the Adige.

The Einspänner horse seems to be unacquainted with oats, but he takes his hay at very short stages of his journey. "Lisa," our comfortable bay mare, was hauled up at the tumble-down little inn of a tumble-down little village, among the vines and olives, for her habitual refreshment. We found the interior comfortable and clean, and the Terlaner wine delicate and good. The gradations of rank among the working-people always struck us as curious. The peasant drivers of our humble drags seemed never to perform the office of groom. The stable-boy of the Gasthaus always takes charge of the feeding and watering, the driver meanwhile taking his quarter liter of red wine, and tipping the hostler

MERAN, FROM THE KUCHELBERG.

with a petty fee, like a gentleman. As the afternoon wore on, our wrinkled and antiquated Jehu grew communicative. He was proud of his age (seventy-two), and he needed little encouragement to wander back to the old days before the time of railroads, when he rode postilion with the diligences over the great post-routes. Of all the hard-riding company to which he had belonged, he alone is left. He seemed to regard himself as the sole remaining monument of a period that has gone never to return. The present, with its swift travel and frequent changes, had no interest for him. He was a dreamy old Rip Van Winkle, with whom the interest of life lay only in the past—until, we being discharged and a return freight from Meran being in order, the present, with its daily bread, came bravely to the front.

CHAPTER VIII.

THE CITY OF THE BELLS.

FEW places along the southern slope of the Alpine range have such a reputation, and few deserve it so well, as the beautiful health-resort of Meran. It lies at the north side of the broad valley of the Adige, close under the shelter of the mountains, and where a bend of the valley carries the protection well around toward the west and east. Its drawback to those in robust health lies in the prominence everywhere given to its restorative characteristics. It is emphatically and conspicuously a "Kurort"—a resort for invalids. On the other hand, many of the appliances for the comfort and entertainment of the sick are of a sort to increase the attractions for the well. Through the town runs the very swift and copious torrent of the Passeier, the banks of which are pleasantly laid out—the sunny side as a winter promenade with sheltered basking places, and the shady side (the summer promenade) with cool retreats and rustic seats under the cover of dense trees and immediately over the rapids. By municipal regulation every guest, whether a *Kur* subject or not, must contribute his weekly fee for the support of the Kursaal, the reading-room, the brass-band, etc. He enjoys them all the more, perhaps, for his sound condition.

No community of Yankees could have turned the whims and fantasies of invalids to better account than have the physicians and the lodging-house keepers of Meran. They seem to have left no curative stone unturned. The grape cure, the whey cure, the cow-milk cure, the sheep-milk cure, water cure, pneumatic cure, and everything which may tickle the fancy of a *malade imaginaire* is worked up to its last pitch; and if faith in means is equal to the abundant and various healing provision, Meran must be a sick man's very paradise. It may, indeed, well be that without any of these artificial accompaniments; for its pure mountain air, its great freedom from wind and dust, and its most equable climate (save in the heat of summer), must combine with its abundant vegetation and its most charming landscape to stimulate nature to her own best restorative processes. Whatever may be its effect upon the sick, I can vouch most heartily for its value to the well, for in few places have I found myself so incited to the best mental and bodily effort as here—not the stimulus and excitement of the higher, crisper mountain air, where one may perhaps be led to tax life's powers inordinately, but a wholesome feeling of energy which fits a man for his best and steadiest work. And not work only, for nowhere else does solid and uninterrupted idleness, the *dolce far niente* of able-bodied and vigorous manhood, come so naturally and leave so little regret. It seems as though time spent in the purest loafing here were really time gained in one's life and memory.

There is no rose without its thorn. Meran, the charming, the sunny, the serene, the health-giving, the life-cheering Meran, has a skeleton in its closet—a skeleton whose dry bones rattle and send a shudder through the nerves, through the very marrow, even of its most robust visitors. How much more must it affect those who are already unstrung by real illness, or, still worse, by fancied invalidism! The deep sleep which its pure fresh air so fosters is broken as with the very falling of the heavens. The tranquil reverie to which its soft acacia shade invites the happy soul is crushed as with the angry voice of devils. The idle saunter beside its noisy, tumbling Passeier Bach, the complete absence of thought to which the most active mind is wooed by its ceaseless swirl, is changed to torture as with the sudden crashing of the very ear-drums. In the still sweet hour of the night and in the broad light of serene day it comes, all unawares and unexpected, and grinds the soul with its harsh turmoil. The enterprising doctors and landlords, and the municipality itself, may do their bravest and best to make their town a haven of health and rest: the priests, whose hand seems turned against all mankind, hold the instrument of torture with a firm grasp, and turn it remorselessly in every suffering breast. By day and by night, in season and out of season, and without rhyme or reason, the "harsh iron clangor of the bells, bells, bells," leaves no rest for body or soul, and makes life here, where all else is calm and quiet and peaceful, a constant alternation of delight and misery. Indolence, reverie, sleep, and all tranquillity are hour by hour jarred and broken by a senseless jangle of brazen noise, as church tower after church tower takes up the oft-repeated alarm, and sends its fiendish vibrations through every unwonted brain.

In all parts of Tyrol the common people adhere to their native characteristics, little influenced by any tide of foreign travel that may flow past them. Nowhere else is this more true than at Meran. The streets are filled with bare-kneed peasants wearing pointed brigand hats, leather breeches, embroidered belts, and broad green suspenders covering them like vests; the shabbiest hats are decked with feathers and flowers, and in the smallest detail of their life and conversation the people are purely and only Tyrolean. They trudge through the streets with heavily laden baskets at their backs, or drive their oddly yoked cows before the clumsy basket-bodied wagons, as their ancestors may have done, and probably did do, a hundred years ago. Surely few other peoples could live thus for years side by side and face to face with money-spending and modern-dressed strangers from all corners of Christendom and remain so entirely unaffected by the contact.

A gentleman to whom I took letters introduced me to one of the largest farmers of the district, who kindly explained to me many details of the methods of cultivation in vogue. The land is extremely fertile. Not only in the valley, but everywhere on the hills and mountain-sides, wherever a little land is free from rock and stone, all the usual Northern farm crops thrive remarkably; and not only these, but the vine, the fig, and the Spanish chestnut as well, save in too high or too exposed situations. The statement, often made, that the lemon grows out-of-doors here and ripens its fruit well is practically a misstatement. It does grow out-of-doors (in the summer-time), and it does ripen its fruit (in warm sunny corners), but the tubs in which it grows have to be moved into glass houses for winter. The land is almost exclusively owned by those who till it. As is always the case with an industrious people farming its own rich land, the whole agricultural community is in a very prosperous condition, and individuals of more than comfortable wealth are by no means rare.

The grape is the most conspicuous crop, and very fair red wine is abundant and cheap. Here, as in much of Northern Italy, the vines are grown on trellises, forming, with their thick foliage, what may best be described as a series of "lean-to" roofs, facing toward the sun, and supported by substantial timber at a height which makes it possible to cultivate Indian-corn under them. Excepting a strip a few feet wide along the rows of vines which is kept clean and well hoed, the intervening ground is occupied by grass or corn, or occasionally by other crops. These vineyards are far more picturesque and attractive than the Lima-bean-like plantations along the Rhine and the Mosel, but it is possible that the dense shading of the whole ground, and the cultivation of grain and grass on the intervening spaces, have much to do with the quality of the wine made, which, though wholesome and palatable, is by no means comparable to wine of a corresponding grade grown in the Rhineland, or in France, where, also, the bean-pole system prevails.

Not only in the valley, but almost equally on the hills, even to a great height, irrigation seems to be the sheet-anchor of the farmer. Water is abundant, and, as the streams are fed from the mountain-tops (often from glaciers), it is constant throughout the season of growth: during the summer months there is never a lack. It is applied to the vines at certain seasons, and to wheat and other grain crops; but the great use of this aid is upon the grass fields, which are copiously flooded about once a week. I have read so much about the processes of irrigation for years, without getting anything like a clear idea of its methods of practical operation, that I shall not attempt any complete description of them here. All of its details are extremely simple. On other than quite flat land the inclination given to the gutters, and the consequent rapidity of the flow, is much greater than I had supposed. Even in the minor channels in a grass field the current runs nimbly on, and the main feeder for a ten-acre field is a babbling brook. The quantity of water used is more than I had thought, but not so great that (by the use of simple methods of storing and occasional discharge) the process might not be adopted very widely in our Eastern States.

I had equally failed to realize the effect to be obtained by thorough irrigation; it is one of those things which "must be seen to be appre-

SCHLOSS TIROL.

ciated." I think that there was hardly a day, from the time when we left Salzburg until we reached Turin, when we did not see irrigation going on, and quite up to the end of September there was hardly a day when we did not see hay-making. In many cases the fourth and sometimes the fifth crop was being cut, and always crops of very respectable yield. If I had learned no other lesson from my journey, I should be amply repaid by the realization it has given me of the great importance of irrigation, on the very small scale as well as on the large; of the almost universal ability to make use of it in one way or another; and of the extreme simplicity and cheapness of its methods.

Our short stay only sufficed for the merest taste of the excursions which are one of the chief attractions of the region. We were told that we might renew every day for a month the delightful experiences in walks and rides and drives which made our sojourn in this land of the vine and the fig and the snow-capped peak seem quite unique among our adventures. The great object of interest—that which is first pointed out by the arriving coachman, which holds the most prominent place among the vanities of the community, and which really deserves all its praise—is the venerable Schloss Tirol. Curious and interesting, but not in itself especially remarkable, it trembles on the border line between ruin and restoration, between neglect and care. Standing on a low hill with an indifferent outlook, it would be no more than any ordinary castle in Tyrol; but planted on the crest of a grand spur of the mountain, 1200 feet above the town, with an outlook up and down the valley of the Adige, it commands a view of unrivalled beauty and variety. To the left, the broad deep trough where the Adige flows to join the Eisach at Botzen is a very paradise of fertility and luxuriance, bordered by the deep green vegetation and the grand red rocks of the porphyry mountains through which it has been cut. Standing sentinel over this valley is the high sharp profile of the Mendel Spitz. To the right, far below, is the tumbling white torrent of the river tearing its way over sharp rocks and among great bowlders, and making a rapid descent of nearly a thousand feet. Farther on stretches the colder and higher but still rich agricultural vale of the Vintchgau. Over and beyond this are seen the Ortler Spitz, the Laaser Glacier, and other white-shrouded members of the Oetz Thal group. The whole transition from the warm and fertile plains of the South to the dead reign of eternal snow is covered by a mere turning of the eyes from left to right.

This old stronghold has the unusual distinction of having given its name to the land to which its possessions were added by the marriage of one of its daughters, Margheretta Maultasch ("Pocket-mouth Meg,") to the reigning count.

Seen from the town, it seems neither very far away nor very high, but I found it a hard hour's scramble for my little mountain horse from the hotel to its dependent village, Dorf Tirol. At first the roadway—paved with long stones laid across it—was almost like a staircase, and its steep course continued so long that when we came out upon the crest we met the curious illusion of water running up hill. The irrigation ditch at the roadside was flowing rapidly toward us, but the sudden change in the grade of the road, and the steep mountain side in front of us, made it hard to realize that we were not descending.

The old lords of Schloss Tirol added to the inaccessible steep on which they founded their fortress the further security of a long tunnel through the hill as an easily defensible entrance, with the inscription, "Imperator Gloriosus Viae istius Autor." The hill is of a sort of hardened clay or softened stone, which is slowly washed away by rain. Here, as in other similar formations, there occurs the curious "phenomenon" of *earth pyramids*. The whole hill-side is flanked by tall pinnacles of earth, each surmounted by a large bowlder. These stones have served as umbrellas to protect the earth under them from the reach of the rain, which has gradually washed away the intervening mass, and left them standing like light-houses with black rocks in the place of lanterns. They are a weird-looking company to come upon at twilight, and one almost hesitates to leave them behind unquestioned as he dives into the dark *Knappenloch*, and rides on among the shades of the Middle-Age bandits and marauders who used to make its vault echo with their riotous jeers, as they rode home, booty-laden, in the old barbarous days of the robber knights.

Another castle, "Schloss Trautmansdorf," to which we were taken quite unawares by a driver who gave us a twilight airing, is, in its very different way, hardly less interesting. It is a real castle of very old date, but it has been preserved from decay, and kept fresh and most habitable. Like all of its contemporaries, it stands on a cliff which is difficult of access.

It was on our way to this castle that we first saw the traditional vineyard guardian of the Tyrol—an example of "costume" in its maddest development—wearing the Tyrolese dress, resplendent with unusual colors, and a huge head-dress of feathers and fox tails and all manner of outlandish decoration. The ancient purpose of this "get-up" was to strike terror into the hearts of grape-loving boys and girls.

More recently its object is said to be the amusement of tourists, the more serious business of protecting property depending on the fact that the guardian carries fire-arms, and has authority to use them.

Notwithstanding all the inviting journey that lay before us, and despite its miserable and incessant bells, the temptation was strong to lay aside all energy and ambition, and to idle away the rest of our holiday in lovely Meran; but it would be as hard to tear ourselves away a month later, and we drove back one fine morning toward Botzen. But what a freight we took with us! what a fund of new-found impressions! what memories of the sweet vale of Meran, and of the mountains and hills, and of the great Vintchgan portal to the high Alpine country where the Oetz Thal group guards the western frontier of Tyrol!

VINEYARD WATCH.

CHAPTER IX.

INTO THE GRÖDNER THAL.

It is curious to observe how a great railway throws into obscurity the country through which it passes. It plants widely separated centres of civilization here and there along its route, but practically it cuts off the wayside villages from intercourse with the world. In the old diligence days every village between Innsbruck and Botzen was familiar with frequent travel; its post-house was enlivened with throngs of passengers, and its special industry or interest had a public upon which to thrive. The Brenner railway has changed all this. The great flood of travel between the north and the south is swept unheeding through the valley, only here and there a tourist, tempted by beauty or romance, halting to awaken once more the echoes which have so long been stilled in the guest rooms of the abandoned Gasthaüser.

Railway travel down the valley of the Eisach is eminently satisfying; the rate of speed is slow enough for one to take in intelligently the most attractive features of the landscape; its halts are frequent enough and long enough for one to study the character and the costumes of the peasants gathered about the stations, and one arrives at Botzen with the satisfactory feeling of having "done" the Brenner. Such was our own impression after repeated trial—an impression which might have lasted through life had we not had occasion to learn its inadequacy. How often, I wonder, has our blissful ignorance blinded us to the best our journeyings have had to offer? In this instance our enlightenment came with the drive from Botzen to Waidbruck on such an afternoon as seems generally to be reserved for the occasion of our expeditions. I say it with bated breath, lest the fates should overhear me and break the charm, and I even whisper the German's cautionary "nicht berufen." But it is a secret which I cannot withhold

ALPEN ROSEN.

from my readers that though those who precede us and those who follow us may be saddened with rain and gloom, when we travel the clouds part before our pathway, and give us sunshine and bright flowers and sweet breezes.

The interest of the road begins immediately on leaving the town. The transition from its sombre streets and its arid piazza to the roses and the vine trellises is instant. Soon the narrow plain is passed, and the great walls of the valley draw closer together, leaving at times barely room for road and river and railway. The mountains grow higher and steeper as the valley narrows, and we penetrate a deep and majestic gorge, winding abruptly to right and to left; now veiled in the shades of twilight, now bursting again into sunshine, filled always with the river's roar, and always rich with a grandeur and beauty which one can no more appreciate from the windows, or even from the observation car of a railway train, than one can appreciate Niagara from the Suspension-Bridge. The form and the substance we may get; but the spirit, the sweetness, the singing of the birds, the fluttering of the leaves, the climbing of the shadows, the life and the still-life—these need the calm and deliberation of slow locomotion. The pleasant greeting of travelling peasants; the clambering of scared goats up the sheer cliffs; the suggestions of the fire-blackened rock where gypsies have camped; the hawk's nest at the top of a dead tree; the strongholds where Hofer and his

A VILLAGE STREET.

hardy men contested the passage of the gorge, as the Romans and the Goths had done before them; the degree to which nature, unheeding all the heroic record of history, has drunk up the wasted blood with the simplest vegetation, and holds all these rocks and ravines as

ST. ULRICH AND THE LANG KOFEL.

pure and fresh as though they had known only the grazing of goats and the soaring of hawks—these come to the apprehension by processes too slow for the railway; not coming, they leave us ignorant of the real essence of remote travel.

The great Gasthaus at which we stopped for hay and coffee is a great ghost-house now, peopled with the memories of the posting days. It still maintains a brave front, gay with flowers, fresh with scrubbing, and always ready for the hurrying throng, which now, alas! sends it but rare and transient representatives. How long this old post-house of Atzwang will continue under its old impetus no one can say. It gets a little foot-weary travel by the high-road, and it is the starting-point for the Kastelruth entrance to the Dolomites; but all this is little for so great a house, and sooner or later "Ichabod" must be written over its door-way.

How many of my readers have ever heard of Waidbruck? If they are told that it is an odd little Tyrol village under the shadow of the mighty Schloss Trostburg, the Roman Acropolis of Sublavione, and the birthplace of Oswald von Wolkenstein, the Minnesinger, and that at the end of its single street a white picket gate opens to let us into the Grödner Thal, they will still have much to learn; for Waidbruck is its only entrance, and though one of the smallest, the Grödner is one of the most curious and most interesting of the valleys of all Tyrol.

Physically, it is a deep score in the steep side of the mountain, eighteen miles long, and 3600 feet higher at its upper than at its lower end. Its population numbers about 3500, which number has not materially varied for ages. Until 1856, this people—always known and always noted—kept up their frequent intercourse with the world, and carried to it their abundant wares over the roughest of mountain footpaths. Now a good carriage-road—a marvel of difficult and costly communal engineering—leads down the steep valley to Waidbruck: for us it led up from Waidbruck. Day had deepened to dusk, and dusk to dark, long before we reached its capital village of St. Ulrich— locally and gutturally "Sanght Hulhrich." The Grödner Bach is a roaring torrent, swirling its way between and around angular rocks, and falling in frequent cascades. The close-lying hill-sides are steep and craggy. Here and there, where a little clearing has been possible, a thrifty farm-house and overflowing barn cling to the acclivity. Everywhere else thick forest clothes the rocky slopes, and through this humming valley we climb higher and higher, past the little village of St. Peter, past occasional level fields, and through still higher and higher forests of pine and black fir, and more frequent clearings and lighted windows. The tall straight pines are trimmed of their side branches to make bedding for cattle, but often branches are left near the top to simulate the cross. These stood in frequent silhouette against the clear sky.

At a bend of the road there rises suddenly before us, high beyond the great fir-clad mountain-side, towering above the very world, and illumined with the golden glow of sunset, the majestic column of the Lang Kofel, the giant king of the Western Dolomites. Separated from its own surroundings, standing out like red gold above the dark forest and against the deep blue, solitary and unmeasured, a shining blaze of glory, it beckons us on, like the pillar of fire by night, to the wonders of the Promised Land. At last the hills part, the starry sky opens, and the sparkling house-lamps of St. Ulrich stretch high up the sides of the broad basin in which the village lies.

At the "White Pony" we found an amiable lisping landlord, and an intelligent and friendly Kellnerin, ready to serve our comfort and to minister to our wants. All the appliances of maps, horses, guides, and luncheons, and wise advice, were at our disposal for the days of our stay, and all the marvels to which the Grödner Thal leads were before us for a choice.

The Grödner Thal itself engaged our earliest interest. Its hidden and so long inaccessible fastnesses caught 2000 years ago the reflux of the tide of Northern barbarians which swept down into Italy only to be driven back by Roman valor, and — save where such a sheltered nook as this caught fragments of the fleeing band — to be wiped from the face of the earth. The eddy of Rhœtian fugitives, resting among these hills, stayed to transmit to our own time the blood, and the hardy personal qualities, and the roots of a language which only here and there besides have escaped total destruction.

The Northmen held to the mountain valleys — the Grödner, the Gader, and the Fassa — and spread out over the intervening hills. The Romans held the fertile lands along the rivers, and guarded the entrance to the valleys. In time, tempted by the accumulated crops and herds, and by the fertile fields of the Rhœtian bands, they encroached upon their domain, usurped their homes, and absorbed their nationality. Hence the mixed race and the mixed speech, which hold their own here better than in the Pyrenees, the Engadine, and elsewhere where the tongue of the troubadours has told of the mingling of Southern and Northern blood, as the two races beat themselves together in mountain warfare. Here, to-day, well within the Austrian domain, and in close intercourse with the world by their active traffic, the descendants of the old Rhœti-Roman heathen hold to their old Romance

COSTUME OF BRIDE IN THE GRÖDNER THAL.

language with the pride of birthright possessors. And not only here, but all the world over, wherever a Grödner has settled, though he may never see his native hills again, he cherishes his native speech, and makes it the mother-tongue of his children.

It is a musical tongue, and a mixed. There must have been soldiers of fortune in those days as in ours, for Spanish and French roots are plenty in the speech, and these could have come to this distant quarter only by the chance fortune of war. Naturally German words have crept into it by contact, and the Italian of the valleys to the south has also made its mark. But these influences have not sufficed to change its fundamental character, any more than neighborhood, religion, and community have modified the fundamental character of the people themselves; the Grödner is still distinct among Tyrolese, and his valley is still unique.

"A Resident"—evidently a priest with a soul above his beads—has recently published a considerable treatise (*Grödlen, der Grödner, und seine Sprache*), which might serve to make the "Ladin," as the people call it, a written language. The composite character is apparent at the very outset.

The numerals are: *Unjn, doi, trëi, catter, cinch, sies, sött, òtt, nuèf, diös; vint* (20), *cënt* (100). Other examples are: *Prim* (1st), *sëcond* (2d), *sëmpl* (single), *dopl* (double).

Jö sonj—I am. *Tu jës*—thou art. *El ëila jè*—he is. *Nous sonj*—we are. *Vo sëis*—you are. *Ëi ëiles jè*—they are. *Jö fòe*—I was. *Jö soy stàt*—I have been. *Jö fòe stàt*—I had been. *Jö savè*—I shall be. *El wo mël dà*—he does not give it to me. *'N mël diŝ*—I am told (one tells me).

Here is the beginning of the parable of the Prodigal Son:

" 'L FIGLIUOL PRODIGO.

"Unj père òva doi fionjs. 'L plu ŝonn và unj di da si père, y diŝ: Père! daŝemë la pèrt, chë më tocca, chè hò la intenzionj de mën ŝi da tlò dëmöz. 'L père partèŝ la ròba, y dà al fi chëll, chë jë tuccòva. 'L fi pòcchè l' hà abu si àrpeŝonj, sën jèl ŝit da tgèsa dëmöz tënj paiŝ dalonè. Ilò hà ël scumënéa a mënè na slötta vita, y in puech temp s' hà 'l döffàtt dutt chëll, chë l'òva giatà da si père."

It is evident at a glance that there is some special source of prosperity in this valley which marks it very distinctly from other parts of Tyrol. It has its own thrifty agriculture and its frugal habits, its untiring industry and its simple mode of life, which go so far to make any people comfortable; but here is more than the comfort of even the best agricultural valleys. A spruce New England air is seen on every hand—in fresh paint, new houses, trim-looking door-yards, and the many minor evidences of good fortune.

The secret of it all is that in the last century the art of *Holzschnitzerei* was introduced among the people, and the manufacture of wooden toys soon became general among them. For a long time this industry has thriven, and has occupied the attention of nearly the

THE WOOD-CARVER.

whole population. Even the children, on coming home from school, sit at the bench and cut busily away at the special object to which the talent of their family has been devoted for generations. It may be horses, or cows, or donkeys, or sheep, or cats, or jointed dolls, or soldiers. It is never a variety. The most skilful cat-maker would stand defeated before the smallest wooden soldier. If the mother and the grandmother made donkeys, tradition and family honor compel the child to make donkeys, and donkeys only, and to transmit the species

TYROLESE COSTUME, VAL SUGANA.

unchanged to succeeding generations. In this way a certain skill, or rather a quick deftness, has been acquired, which has led to most abundant production. Ordinarily the quality of the work is extremely rude; it rarely leads to anything like artistic performance; but it has sufficed to fill the whole civilized world with the painted wooden toys of the Grödner Thal.

For a century or so these wares found their way to market in the packs of the peddlers, who regularly visited all the principal fairs of Europe. Later, dealers in toys established themselves at St. Ulrich, and bought the whole product for ready money. The peddlers turned their attention to other merchandise, and to-day furnish a very large quota of the pack-carriers who peddle the lighter appliances of domestic life.

With the attachment to their homes which is characteristic of all Tyrolese—and, indeed, of all mountaineers—the profit of their traffic, saved with rare economy, generally serves to increase the comfort of their native homes, and to improve the condition of their families. In this way, as well as directly, the toy industry has been a chief element in the prosperity of the people. Since the road has been opened the shipment of toys in large packages has been carried on directly from the valley, which is visited by buyers from most distant lands. We saw huge cases marked for Spain, Sydney, and Brazil. Along the valley road and on all the mountain paths we constantly met women and children and old men with back-baskets filled with freshly painted toys, all bound for Herr Purger's great Noah's ark of a warehouse.

It indicates what frugal life in Tyrol implies when we find that the evidence of marked prosperity in the Grödner Thal, as contrasted with small valleys where agriculture is the only resource, is chiefly due to a petty industry which brings a return of less than one dollar per week for each member of the population. This is supplemented by the savings of the wandering peddlers, and there is a certain amount of domestic weaving which ekes out the income of many a family; but when all is reckoned, we shall find that the art of money-saving has been a larger factor in the accumulation of Grödner wealth and comfort than the art of money-making.

The wood-carving is not entirely confined to the rude toy-making in which nearly the whole peasantry is employed. There are many carvers of Madonnas and saints—some of them skilful—who find their market wherever the Catholic Church exists. The chief dealer in St. Ulrich has some examples of artistic work, inferior, however, to that of Innsbruck. We visited a carver's shop where an old man and his wife were busy with church effigies, large and small. They were extremely deft and clever in the handling of their many tools, and in the precision with which they cut to the exact line where the desired expression lay hidden. We selected an unfinished group—"The Education of the Virgin"—and sat by while the grave and responsible maternal look was developed in St. Anna's face, and a real learner's interest and curiosity were awakened in the Virgin. It is a rude little block, and we declined to have it "finished;" but it is full of ex-

A MOUNTAIN PORTER.

pression. Made without model or drawing, it is real, honest sculptor's work. The trained eye of these people sees the statue in the unhewn wood, and they know how to cut away the chips which conceal it.

During our wanderings we made quite a complete collection of photographs of Tyrolese costumes, some of them belonging to this valley. The habit with regard to dress varies with the locality. Here and in the Ziller Thal the every-day gear is not especially marked, the full costume being reserved for Sundays and festivals. In other valleys, at Meran and at Berchtesgaden, the "world's" dress is hardly worn at all by the peasants. Everywhere the climate seems peculiarly adapted to the growth of flowers and feathers in the hat-bands of men of all classes and of all nations. It is especially pleasing to see a staid, smooth-shaven Englishman, who at home would reprehend the wearing of anything less than a stiff hat, unbend his rigid lines, deck himself with light and rolling felt, and sport a cock feather or a bunch of Edelweiss at his crown. It is good, too, to see his sidelong glances at the mirrors, and the little wreath of pleasure that winds about his lips at the thought of such rare indulgence.

The costumes are everywhere interesting. Many of them depend mainly on color, and cannot be well reproduced in engraving; but others, as those of Val Sugana and the Sarn Thal, are of curious form. Most of them are very old, and they are all worn with traditional pride.

Although the Grödner Thal is the seat of a special industry, its agriculture has all the minuteness and care of that of the rest of Tyrol. The wood-carving does not supplant, it only supplements, the usual work of the farmer. The land is good, irrigation is universal, and the little hill-side fields are very productive. There is only the one wagon-road, which leads to the head of the valley, with a few side routes to the lateral gorges, where rude mountain carts—with wheels in front and runners behind—are occasionally used. Nearly the whole transportation of hay and grain from the fields to the commodious barns is over foot-paths, immense loads being laboriously carried on the shoulders of the people, sometimes in large coarse sheets, sometimes in baskets, and sometimes on a sort of rack resting on the head and the back.

CHAPTER X.

A DAY ON THE SEISSER ALP.

St. Ulrich is the best point from which to visit the Seisser Alp, and the Seisser Alp is deemed the best worth visiting of all the high pastures of Tyrol. Its fir-grown brink forms the southern horizon of the Grödner Valley for many a mile, and its great eastern barrier, the Lang Kofel, is nowhere more imposing than here, flanked as it is by the grand Dolomite bank of the Meisules which incloses the head of the valley.

I have been able thus far to withhold my personality and my personal belongings from the attention of my readers. I can do so no longer. The day's adventure which I am about to describe owes some of its important features to my relations with the gentler sex. I am a married man, and my wife, who is large, and whose name is Jane, is the constant companion, the guide — and the check — of my travels. Jane is a person of rare virtues, of quick intelligence, of great force of character, and a conscientious disciplinarian. In my case, if ever, the sound motto is true, that "Ce que femme veut, Dieu le veut." I cherish no hope for long, I indulge no ambition openly, which has not had the stamp of her approval. The well-regulated, middle-aged current of my life owes to her sage judgment its even course. The deviations into which, unguarded, I am sometimes led, are bent quickly and gently back to the straight path by her soft firm touch. It needs not to be stated that my walk and conversation are unimpeachable.

Jane is in all things intellectual and spiritual my superior. In the art of equitation she is my inferior. Here is my one triumph over her, and henceforth, when I see evidence of undue assumption, I hope that reference to the Seisser Alp will bring her meekly back to her just level.

A DAY ON THE SEISSER ALP. 87

THE LANG KOFEL, FROM THE SEISSER ALP.

As we first entered the hall of the White Pony we noticed a side-saddle whose generous measurements seemed to set at rest certain doubts with which we had contemplated the ascent to the flowery meadows.

The morning after our arrival a stalwart black horse—Moro—built after the model of the knights' horses in the days of iron armor, stood at the door, his broad loins caparisoned with that noble hog-skin. I never hesitate to put up a nimble girl who floats to the saddle with a touch, but I allowed Moro to be brought along-side a carpenter's bench, whence my sturdy Jane sat down upon him with ease and dignity. The stout back settled to an unaccustomed sway, but nothing broke, and we marched bravely out on our venturesome way. Being mounted, inconvenient doubts began to arise as to dismounting. One who rides for the first time in twenty years cannot ride all day without intermission. Having dismounted, how to mount again? We were bound for a region where carpenters' benches do not prevail. The question annoyed us —I say "us" from sympathy— until we had gone quite up to the neighboring village of Santa Kristina, and had left the highroad to cross the brook and take the bridle-path which leads obliquely up the mountain-side. Was it a steep path? Ask Jane if it was steep. I see her now clutching that horn with her bruised knee, that mane with her weary fingers, that apparent summit of the climb with her anxious eyes. I am guiltless of all wish for revenge; our small by-gones may be by-gones; old scores soon heal in my wonted heart; but if there *had* been reckonings to settle, how that long and weary hill would have fed my heart with satisfaction!

TYROLESE COSTUME, BARN THAL.

At last the zigzag course—each zig harder than the last zag—brought us out upon a plain, an inclined plain, beyond whose distant rim projecting tree-tops told of level ground. Our guide—voluble in Ladin, but halting in German—was a mute spectator of our woe. The only comfort he could suggest was a cooling spring in the edge of the Alp where we might rest and be consoled. In time we had finished our first two hours' travel, and were fairly on the first pastures of the Seisser Alp, 2000 feet above St. Ulrich, and only 4000 below the summit of the Lang Kofel, which rose like a huge fortress tower almost across our path.

The spring reached, my own thirsty lips lay easily over its brimming flow; but the memories of even twice twenty years gave Jane no precedent for this method of imbibition, and she sat like Tantalus at the brink of the flood without the power to drink. My life has been marked by many acts of conjugal devotion, but the humility with which I carefully ate out a hard-boiled egg from its shell with the point of my penknife, and filled the tiny cup again and again, until the cravings of my bride had been sated, must stand recorded against the day when I shall need special indulgence. We drank and we ate, and we held council. We stood at the entrance of a land whose praises had long been sung in our ears — a land of many cattle, of flowers uncounted, and flowing with a very tide of the richest milk.

The air was filled with the melody of tinkling bells, the sun rode warm in the September sky, and the smoke of Sennerin's huts floated over the trees. To go on or to turn back — that was the question which racked us. The other descent was not harder than the way by which we had come, but it lay miles on beyond the hills and valleys we had come to see. Too wise for that, I ventured no advice, but I rejoiced in her stout heart when my tried wife decided to mount her steed and follow her venturesome day to its end. Even a woman's decision is not always achievement, and to place that form again in its seat needed more than mental exertion. The fences, the bar-ways, the stumps, and the stones which we tried and found inadequate, it would be tedious to recount. At last we succeeded, the guide and I, by dint of our combined pushing, in forcing Moro close along-side a sufficient rock, and in holding him there until his charge was seated.

On level ground all went well, and down-hill work was easy enough, but the frequent steep climbs, as we came out of gullies and up the banks of deeply furrowed brooks, tested the endurance of that fond frame, and lined the kind face with anxious thought as to the coming hours.

Yet even personal inconvenience and dread could not dull us to the glories by which we were surrounded. For miles away to the south and west, accentuated by dark tree-filled valleys, rolled the green billows of this glorious summer pasture, dotted with cattle, radiant with wild flowers, and traversed by the slow-moving shadows of clouds. Hundreds of huts and barracks shelter its people and its hay, and thousands of cattle feed over its unfenced expanse.

The Lang Kofel, the Plat Kogel, and the jagged little peaks of the Horse Teeth guard its eastern side, and the Rosengarten and the ponderous horned reef of the Schlern wall out the world at the south. One is more in the heart of the Dolomites at Cortina, but nowhere more impressed with their characteristic and solitary grandeur than here.

We had counted largely upon milk for our food in this excursion, and we made our next halt at the hut of a Sennerin who combines the entertainment of chance travellers with her dairying industry. We took seats on a porch at the shady side of the house, and at a table where two cow-herds sat facing each other, eating "Schmarn"* and milk from the same earthen basin. A similar basin of milk was set between us, and two iron spoons were furnished us. Preceding writers on Tyrolean travel had emphasized the badness of the food, and a thoughtful friend in New England had kindly urged on our acceptance a dyspeptic preparation of parched and sweetened wheat meal with which to supplement our insufficient provender. This had lain unused and unneeded in our satchel all the way from home. Its time had now come, and we soaked it, according to prescription, in our milk, eating to the memory of friends who fancy there are mountains in Massachusetts.

The cow-herds, finishing their meal, rose from the table, crossed themselves, stood facing the east, and devoutly repeated a long prayer, with due genuflection and bowing of the head, and then trudged away to their work. The woman of the house showed us her simple sum-

---

* A compound of grease and Indian-meal.

mer dairy and her loom, inspected our novel outfit, and sent us on our way rejoicing. She could spare no hay for our horses, and we marched on to the hut of a bald and barefooted little old man, who made us welcome, and stood in blue-eyed wonder as we told him we had come from beyond the great sea. His loft not only fed our beasts, it fur-

COSTUME OF THE DUX THAL.

nished Jane a fragrant couch, where for two hours she slept away the weariness of her saddle, and awoke refreshed for her further ride.

This was my first Alpine dairy, and a very good example it was of the summer home of the mountain cow-tender, with an open hearth in the smoky front-room, and a comfortable-looking bed in the milk-room. The old man makes both butter and cheese from a herd of a dozen cows, and his employer sends regularly from Kastelruth to fetch the product to market.

For five months the cows are kept here in the mountains, and during the hay-making season the whole vast Alp is gay with throngs of young men and women, with work and music and dancing. When we saw it the harvest was over, and only the cattle-tenders were left. In another month it would be quite deserted, its great elevation — from 5000 to 7000 feet—subjecting it to early killing frosts. It is a compact rolling plateau of the richest grass land, varied by occasional woods, thirty-six miles in circuit, and belongs mainly to the neighboring communes of Seiss and Kastelruth.

We took up our homeward march about the middle of the afternoon, and struck across over the hills toward the rough cart track which leads down through the wild Saltaria Gorge into the Gröden Valley some distance below St. Ulrich. Jane's comfort did not increase—indeed, her sufferings did not cease—but she is a woman, and when she had given to her sensations the varied articulate expression with which she is so richly gifted, she relapsed into her most eloquent condition of silent and enduring fortitude, which, more than any spoken words, tears my heart with the consciousness that I have, all by my own blundering, masculine obtuseness, led her a sad and sorry dance, whose last echoes I am far from having heard.

However, the magnificent view we gained of the far-away snow-fields of the Oertler Mountains, bordered at one side by the great gray precipice of the Schlern, and at the other by the green slope and pine-clad crest of the Puflatsch, could be trusted to remain and delight her memory long after the bruising and straining of the ride had been forgotten; so I was sure of my final recompense. Then, too, with all her greater qualities, she has feminine traits which are always available, under skilful manipulation, to divert her attention from her own discomfort. Babies, dogs, cats, and donkeys hold the key to her most hidden heart, and even horses are extremely useful in emergency. I have never found that horses are especially fond of clover heads. Offered a handful of grass containing them, it is not these which they first select. Yet so firm is her conviction that a tuft of red clover blossoms is the last desire of the horse's palate, that I can calm her wildest moods by indulging her in this pet fiction. How she would ever have made the long and really trying descent to the valley, had I not kept her Moro supplied with these talismanic tidbits, I do not know. Thus diverted, she came blandly down, and I laid her bruised form, sore with seven hours' riding, on the best feather-bed at the Pony, happy in the thought that I had mitigated to a marked degree her unexpressed chidings for my ill-judged exploit.

The next expedition I made by myself with a guide. Two hours of slow driving took us up the steep road through Santa Kristina and Santa Maria to Plan, at the very head of the valley, where at a height of over five thousand feet a curly-headed Rip Van Winkle keeps a pleasant-looking inn and a small farm. While my horse was being fed we sat on the balcony together, and chatted about his possessions and his easy-going life. It was with real glee that he lay back in his chair and pointed to a little army of women and girls, gay with all the colors of Grödner clothing, reaping merrily in his small grain-field. He was evidently in the early stages of inherited prosperity, and life was all "happy-go-lucky" for him. Hidden away in this obscure corner of the world, he is likely to be his own most frequent customer, and his sturdy Gretchen already shrugs her shoulders over his unthrifty ways.

My destination, the Coll di Rondella, was an hour and a half away —up in the sky. It is a "compromise" ascent, an ascent to be made in the saddle, where a guide is taken only as a matter of courtesy, an easily reached eminence which suffices to save the reputation of one who visits a mountain region without tempting the Fates by crag scrambling. It suited my own ambition precisely, and I rode up the steep, rough bridle-path with the feeling that I was performing an easy and pleasant duty. Much of the route lies over the broken Alps, between the Lang Kofel and the Meisules—here close neighbors and infinitely grand—and touches nearly the summit of the Sella Pass. Close beside the pass rises a steep mamelon of a hill, grass-grown to its summit, and so much lower than the great peaks about it that it seems only recently to have attracted the notice of travellers. Its last acclivity is too steep for riding, and it is trying to unhardened legs. I was beginning to toil and blow when the guide taught me quite a new use of that noble animal the horse. Hitherto I had regarded his tail as a merely ornamental, or at best as a fly-whipping, member. I now, for the first time, learned its value as a tow-line. Grasping it with both hands, I found it an efficient mitigator of my labor, and I came fresh and happy to the top.

The sky was clear, and I stood literally amidst the glories of the

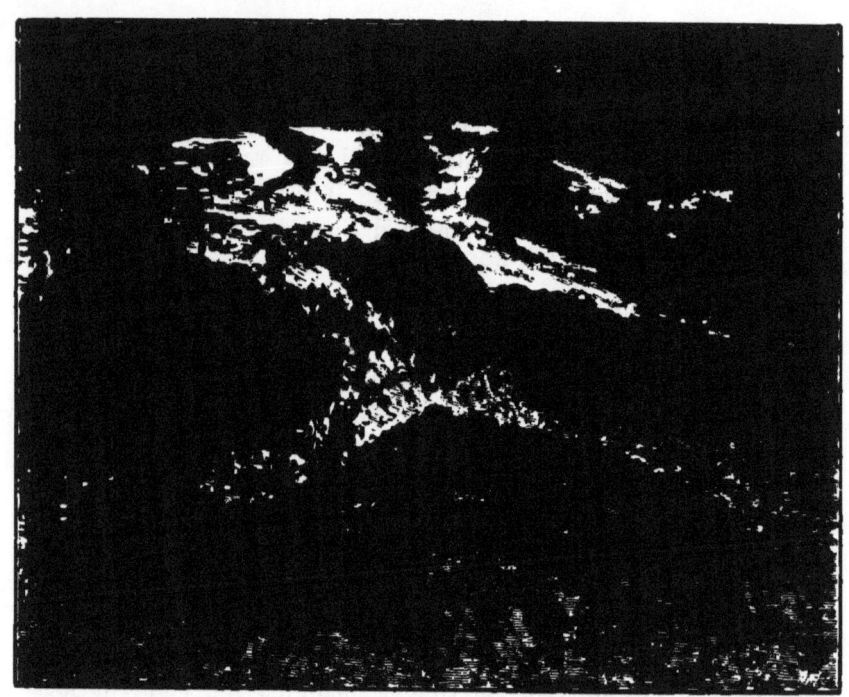

THE GLACIER OF MARMOLATA.

upper world. The tiny houses of Campidello nestled in the sunshine far down in the Fassa Thal. A little stretch of dull Alpine grass and moss lay all about; and beyond this, to the far-away horizon on every side, was spread out a turmoil and wilderness of mountain more magnificent and impressive than any sight that had ever greeted my eyes before. The vast grim glacier of the Marmolata was close before us, the conical peak of Tofana shut out the Ampezzo Valley, and the giants of Tyrol, from Vorarlberg to the Carinthian border, from the Ober Pinzgau range to the Venetian Alps, stood in thick array on every side. With a later and more difficult experience in my mind, I commend the Coll di Rondella to those who would see this company of mountains all unshorn of their grandeur, their majesty measured by the stern scale of the overtopping Lang Kofel and the Titanic peaks of the Sella, which stand out a full half mile above their fringe of stunted pines. Its easy climb was the best-rewarded excursion that I made in Tyrol.

The constant down-hill drive to Waidbruck in broad daylight revealed the superb details of this most charming of mountain roads, which our evening ascent had hardly more than suggested. It is as picturesque as the Wissahickon and as grand as the White Mountain Flume, and everywhere noisy with the rush of the mad Grödner Bach, which pours its foaming flood through a channel piled with huge rocks. Its scenery is unique among mountain valleys, as are its people among the secluded communities of the far-away corners of the world.

CHAPTER XI.

AT THE FOOT OF THE GREAT RANGE.

We had regarded the Puster Thal too lightly. One is disposed to consider a valley where a railway has been built as necessarily tame and unromantic. Even our knowledge of the wild route of the Brenner road had not chastened us of this heresy.

The Puster Thal is in its way unsurpassed. Beginning at Franzensfeste, 2500 feet above the sea, it climbs on to a height of over 4000 feet at the Toblach plain, and thence descends to 2250 feet at Lienz. It is the main stem of the chief system of valleys in South-eastern Tyrol; the entrance to the Pfunder Thal, Gader Thal, Taufers Thal, Antholzer Thal, Pragser Thal, Höllensteiner Thal, Sexen Thal, Villgratten Thal, Isel Thal, Möll Thal, Kalser Thal, Virgen Thal, and Tauren Thal.

> "And these vales have smaller vales,
> And these have vales to feed 'em."

They are the main arteries of a vast net-work of mountain valleys reaching up to the region of the scantiest summer grass, peopled with eager farmers, who cling to the last patch of ground, no matter how high or how steep, which promises even the most meagre means of subsistence.

Whence these peoples came it would be hard to trace, even through their dialects, and the dialect sometimes changes in the same valley. Like the Grödner Thalers, they are probably the descendants of the mixed crowds of refugees who were stranded here when the Northern armies were driven back by the Romans. Whatever they are in origin, they have become genuine Tyrolese, with all the acquired characteristics of a hardy mountain race. They have yielded to the conditions which have everywhere moulded the natures of their fellow-countrymen. Yet the inherent germ has not been changed, blood and tradition still assert their force, and the distinctions which are indicated by speech and by costume have their root in fundamental distinctions of character.

It adds very much to the interest of all Tyrolean travel, which looks beneath the mere surface show of scenery and dress, to inquire into the composite influences by which mankind has been made what it is in these valleys, what original traits still assert their vitality, and what force "environment" has exerted to mould different races toward a common type.

Physically, the Puster Thal yields nothing in grandeur or in interest to its most noted rivals. It is quite different—different from them all—and it would be senseless to attempt a detailed comparison between it and them. It is idyllic, grand, pastoral, gorge-like, broad, simple, and romantic by turns, but even in its simplest phases it is never without the charm of the finest mountain surroundings. Its northern side valleys run quite up into the heart of the Grosser Venediger and Gross Glockner range, and tap its glaciers for their brooks. At the south it skirts along the outlying spurs of the Dolomites, which lift their mysterious fronts far over its bordering hills, and shed into its bosom the uncanny light with which they reflect each setting sun.

Beautiful though the Puster Thal is in itself, it borrows even greater beauty from the branches which it sends back into the mountains. Every point is full of interest. It has no considerable industry save its agriculture, and a few quiet small towns scattered here and there suffice for its commerce. Yet Amthor's *Tyrol Guide* devotes nearly a hundred closely printed pages to little else than an abbreviated cataloguing of what it has to offer to the tourist. A whole busy summer would not nearly suffice for the exploration of most enticing attractions, to which it is the principal entrance.

It served in our case as the road to the Ampezzo Valley, and it attracted us by another object of pilgrimage, interesting in every corner of the world where the English language is read.

William and Mary Howitt—the most married names of our literature—have long set up their summer tent at Dietenheim, at the mouth of the Tanfers Thal. Thither we went to claim one ray of their genial sunshine before their declining day shall have set forever. In a fine old château, from which the high-well-born owners have fled, and which now serves the modest uses of a farm-house, they have taken the handsomer apartments for their cool and quiet retreat.

WILLIAM HOWITT.

Their salon might be, for its size, the Rittersaal of a castle, but it is filled now with flowers and fresh air and smiling light, and with the simple furniture of the temporary home, where these genial, active, and happy octogenarians speed away the mellow days of summer with their books and their friends. One gets from an hour passed with them an insight into the happy possibilities of ripe old age, and looks forward with a fresh interest to the time when one's own long downhill of life shall bring good and sweet reward for the work of the busier years. We certainly turned away from their door forever happier for the light they had shed across our path.

The Taufers Thal—a broad flat plain reaching back into the foot of the snow mountains—had just now been the scene of a geologic event which spread wide disaster through its community. The same deluge of rain which did such havoc in the Ziller Thal, on the opposite slope of the mountain, so saturated the hanging bank of one of the narrower gorges of this valley that its added weight tore the earth away from the rock, and it fell, in an enormous land-slide, forming a high dam across the chasm. The waters rose behind the barrier and accumulated in a vast lake, burying deeply the farms and houses of the people. Rising to the brink of the dam, it poured over the soft and unstable deposit. It was like "the beginning of anger." The soft earth melted away, and the whole accumulated flood came pouring down into the plain, dealing destruction on every hand, washing away field and forest, sweeping long-established houses from the face of the earth, covering miles of cultivated land with the barren wash of the hills, and filling the valley with desolation. Unlike the people of the Ziller Thal, these peasants had little accumulated wealth, and their misfortune is absolute. It will take generations of toil and frugality to repair the damage of this swift calamity.

European communities have one great advantage of which we are deprived, in the fact that they had been long established before the advent of the railway, and had provided themselves with good and permanent carriage roads. There runs through the Puster Thal, all the way from Franzensfeste to Lienz, a smooth, hard, macadamized road, over which the post-service used to be performed, and which, now that through travel and transportation have taken to the rail, remains as a last connecting link between the thrifty villages with which it is lined. It is a most charming tourist's drive-way, and its many old posting inns are still ready with their comfortable cheer. Mühlbach, Brunneck, Toblach, Innichen, and Lienz, and the many minor villages, offer each its own attractions, and each is surrounded by its peculiar points of interest.

With two good horses and a travelling-carriage for the main journey, and saddles for side excursions, a congenial couple might find in this vale of beauty the means for passing the pleasant months of the year in most serene and satisfying enjoyment. The notable wonders

LIENZ, PUSTER THAL.

of the country are available to the more rapid tourist; but time, the chiefest element of a real appreciation of such characteristic scenery and of such a characteristic population, can be secured only by the compulsory slowness of driving or walking. Travellers by rail are never absorbed by the country through which they pass. Speed carries one unheeding over the surface of all local life, and scenes change too swiftly for us to get the local flavor. The best of all is to walk, to halt and chat at the doors of peasants' houses, to dawdle away the hours at way-side Gasthänser, and to burrow slowly into the tranquil spirit of the people. But Jane is averse to walking, and I am glad to compromise with the Einspänner. I get the compensation that we need not halt for every baby of this prolific land, nor pull clover heads for every sage donkey that we meet.

It is not every valley that ends so charmingly as does the Puster Thal, which spreads out into a broad and fertile plain at Lienz—a mountain-embowered Arcadia, quite at the far end of the active world —through which a railway passes, it is true, but where even the current of tourists is unknown.

Few valleys, too, end at the gates of such magnificence; for at Lienz is the entrance to the wild pass of Heiligenblut, where a veritable phial of the blood of the Crucifixion works its miracles at the high altar, and whence starts the rugged climb to the Franz Joseph Höhe, and that greatest of all Tyrol peaks, the Gross Golckner, which dominates the whole land.

Where else than at Tolbach can one step out from the door of a good modern hotel and stroll into such a deep slit in the mountain-side as that which opens the way to the very heart of the Ampezzo Dolomites?

CHAPTER XII.

THE PORTALS OF THE DOLOMITES.

At the edge of South-eastern Tyrol, within an area of forty miles by thirty, stand all of the great peaks of the dolomite formation: it is *par excellence* the region of the dolomite Alps. It has been known to geologists since Dolomieu, at the close of the last century, described the mineral which was to bear his name, and identified it with this mountain formation. So far as secular travel is concerned, the district remained practically unknown until the publication of the work of Gilbert and Churchill describing their explorations of 1861-63. Other more popular writers followed them, applying to the remarkable features of the region more or less appropriate expressions of description and admiration.

The glimpse of the Rosengarten from Botzen, the bald head of the Lang Kofel as seen from St. Ulrich, and the majestic broadside of this rock and the Platt Kofel, the jagged spikes of the Ross Zähne, and the flat ridge and sharp horn of the Schlern, which bound the Seisser Alp on the east and south, had given us an entirely characteristic and comprehensive idea of the varied formation. These were majestic sentinels guarding the outposts of the stronghold. Far up in the Puster Thal, spectre crests, under the rosy light of fading day, beckoned us on to the citadel. We entered the portals at Toblach, through the grand defile which gives entrance to the Ampezzo Valley. Before us, a sharp high peak, almost over our heads, shut out the morning sun, which gave a fringe of silver to every twig of the firs and bushes at its top, and poured down into the valley in opaline streams of light. After passing the Toblacher-See the walls of the valley grew steeper, the bare mountain-tops rose higher, and we penetrated into the very heart of the grand peaks—streaked with red and yellow, seamed with angry scars and fissures, and set in pines almost black in their sombre hue.

Near the first habitation, a comfortable inn at Landro, the Höllenstein, with Monte Piano and the Drei Zinnen, stood high before us. Beyond the Dürren-See rose the tilted masses of Monte Cristallo, which the lake mirrors like a glass. At Schluderbach another way-side inn is busy with coming and going travellers. Before it rises the Croda Rossa, one of the highest of the dolomites, its precipices stained with broad bright red patches. Gilbert says that it is "streaked as with the red drip of a mighty sacrifice."

THE INN AT LANDRO.

The road has risen constantly from Toblach, and almost uninterruptedly from Botzen. At its highest point it is very nearly 5000 feet above the level of the sea, having insensibly consumed nearly one-half of the nominal height of the highest mountains of the region, carried us nearly to the limit of gradual slope and of vegetation, and brought us close to the barren rock and precipitons walls, and filling our lungs with the clear and invigorating air of a high Alpine valley.

We had come far enough to compare our preconceived ideas of the dolomites with the majestic reality with which we were surrounded. We were in no respect disappointed—far from it; but we were made to realize the inadequacy of language and of human imagery to convey a true impression of these scenes. "Cathedrals," "flying-but-

SCHLUDERBACH AND THE CRODA ROSSA.

tresses," "watchtowers," "lions conchant," "bastions," "needles," "bayonets," and the multiform expressions leading to a comparison with the insignificant works of man, seemed only a feeble attempt to define and measure in language created for worldly things a grandeur which is really inexpressible, and which even requires a certain familiarity to be appreciated by the eye which gazes upon it.

Through a clear air and under a cloudless sky the mountaintops all seem unduly near. It needs the half-concealment and the shadow of floating clouds to throw them back to their real distance and to lift them to their real height. Here, even more than among mountains of ordinary form, partial concealment and the vast contrast between nearness and distance best develop the grandeur of the greater peaks. The Lang Kofel nowhere seems so far, so large, and so high as when its pale, clear-cut, yellowish shaft reaches up far above and far behind the dark and sharply defined fir-clad mountains which shut in the Gröduer Thal. Monte Pelmo, as it lifts its great head into the distant sky far beyond the serrated top of the high Becco di Mezzodì, is vastly more impressive in magnitude and in elevation than when its whole side has come into view. Something of the effect may be due to the mystery of suggestion, but more to the fact that we need the majestic scale of an intertervening mountain to measure rightly such enormous heights and masses.

I shall refrain from all attempt to express in words the remarkable and various forms and effects of the dolomite peaks, further than to say that in their general characteristics—and there are many exceptions even to this—they are full of sharp angles, fantastic serrations, and knife-like edges. So little does the eye appreciate relative distance that two mountains rising one behind the other, and having a wide valley between them, look like a single slope, until a cloud, filling the valley, brings the nearer summit into clear relief. In certain lights, and especially in the gray following the sunset, they frequently look like vertical sheets of gray pasteboard, with a jagged edge standing in sharp profile against the lighter sky; again, they seem a mass of cold gray stone rising high out of the fields and forests, pitiless, cheerless, baleful, and cruel; again, under strong sunlight, they are modelled with infinite sharp shadow, and mellowed with the warmest creamy and ruddy glow, even the broad blackened patches of the older exposures assuming a warm blue tone. The first impression received may well belie all that we have read, for aspect, medium, light and shadow, and all the infinite variations of atmospheric effect, change the tone, the feeling, and almost the very form itself. What we see to-day we shall not see to-morrow; a description true now may never be true again. It seems to me that this constant and endless change of effect is more characteristic of the scenery than any other of its peculiarities.

The same forms are scattered through the calcareous mountains as far as the plain of Venetia and Lombardy. They look down upon Riva from the precipitous west wall of Garda; they haunt the traveller by the Lecco arm of Lake Como, they appear again at Lugano, they are conspicuous in the Pyrenees, and they are a very frequent accompaniment of limestone ranges the world over, but only here in Tyrol have they their full characteristic effect.

CHAPTER XIII.

CORTINA D'AMPEZZO.

NEAR the head of the Ampezzo Valley, in the ganglion centre from which reach out the various systems of mountain and valley toward the north, south, east, and west, high up among the barren rocks, and close to their frowning and beetling and broken edges, there exists a combination of direction, of exposure, of distorted form, of light and shade, and of atmospheric condition, which turns the weird kaleidoscope from hour to hour, and produces the unusual and changing effects with which literature has grappled so much in vain.

It is, no doubt, safe to say that the rapid growth of the Dolomites in popular favor is founded on real merit, and that it will continue and increase. An envious admirer of the superb landscapes of North Tyrol said to us, half contemptuously: "Yes, the Dolomites are in fashion now." While yielding nothing to him in appreciation of his beloved native hills, which must ever hold their own as being unrivalled in their own way, I must freely confess that the doubts with which I first entered the Ampezzo Valley have all been dispelled, and that I accept the wonders and glories it has to offer with unreserved and unstinted admiration. They are glories and they are wonders which enchant and which glow the more as familiarity brings us acquainted with their secret spirit. With this feeling, it is almost amusing to hear the fear expressed that the region will soon become "hackneyed" and overrun with tourists, like Switzerland. I trust it to withstand, all untarnished, the gaze of clouds and generations of tourists and pleasure-seekers. The ants which burrow its hill-sides and build pitfalls for unwary feet affect as much these grand old rocks above them as will all the men and women who may come to clamber about their lower slopes, and marvel over their inaccessible steeps. *Per*

CORTINA AND MONTE TOFANA.

contra, increased travel will lead to the opening of roads and footpaths, to the diffusion of comfort, to the decrease of discomfort, and to ease of access; still more, the travellers will be made happy and healthier; and, if man continues an imitative animal, here and there one may carry back to his remote home a knowledge of certain manners at table which do not now obtain there. The adherents of exclusiveness in the enjoyment of mountains may rest happy in the hope that no railroad will ever climb the high Ampezzo Pass, for neither commercial nor military needs indicate such danger.

It seems altogether likely that Cortina will remain the central point of interest of the district. It is a snug little Italio-German town in the midst of the straight stretch of the valley at its broadest and richest part, four thousand feet above the sea, and most delicious in climate—without the chill of the Engadine or the heat of more enclosed valleys. It is a climate where exercise is a delight, where sleep is a revelation, and where appetite finds wholesome stimulus, and gives good sauce to abundant food.

Happily this is not a guide-book, and I am not called upon to discuss the relative merits of the Golden Star and the Black Eagle. The tidy and still fine-looking sisters Barbaria, and the lusty and stalwart brothers Ghedina, have and will continue to have their warm adherents and their plentiful patrons. It is not as advice to my readers—only as a tribute to merit—that I commend the Aquila Nera for its open situation, its airy and generally large rooms, and the Teutonic profusion of its table.

It is not often that the Kellnerin of a hotel, good and obliging though she may be, can claim more than passing notice; but Filomena, the earnest-faced, calm-minded, gentle, and unflagging maiden who holds the comfort of each guest and the welfare and mainspring of the whole establishment in her active hands and willing heart, deserves more than thanks from all to whose wants and to whose whims she has uncomplainingly ministered.

Doubtless at the Stella d'Oro or at the Croce Bianca we should have fallen in with the varied tide of human nature by which the experiences of the traveller are always so much enriched, but at the Ghedinas' not only did we have the advantage of the society of most agreeable compatriots, and of some English of the rarer and better sort, and of cultivated Germans, but we renewed our experience of what may be called the "absorptive" type of English tourist—those who create every landscape before which they stand, whose presence fills every room into which they come, and whose ceaseless self-consciousness is an oppression to all about them. Surely, with all their faults, other nations do not inflict upon the modest travelling world the equals of these loud-talking, all-pervading, ever-prominent, and egregiously wooden persons. They are typical, but happily they are rare. It is but fair to say that they are as objectionable to their fellow-countrymen as to others. Cortina was rich in examples of the type. The world can hardly furnish a grander road for driving or for walking than the Ampezzo highway from the mouth of the Val Grande to Cortina. It was recommended to one of these gentry as the best way home from an excursion. He replied, in loud, leaden tones: "It is poorish business to walk on a highway, you know." Another had crossed the Fedaia Pass. It is one of the grand excursions of the Dolomites. He characterized it as "a remarkably jolly pass," and he had "made" it in an hour less than Ball's time. This was all that he had to say about it, but he was voluminous on the subject of a mistake

FRESCO ON THE OUTSIDE OF THE AQUILA NERA.

concerning his boots, and a "thorough-going raw" on his heel. He reappeared at intervals during several days, and we were kept advised as to the condition of his "raw." Instances might be multiplied, but these will suffice.

Two of the brothers Ghedina are artists of considerable merit. Across the street from the hotel is a "Dependence" containing a dozen or more rooms. The outside of this building, which is new, is being entirely and very artistically frescoed—the front with very good allegorical pictures after the manner of Kaulbach, and the south side with really excellent representations of Tyrolean domestic life. Here and there, in out-of-the-way places, appear various smaller pictures, one room being decorated with clever imitations of framed photographs, line engravings, and cheap chromos—a whimsical conceit capitally carried out.

The people of Cortina are simple, industrious, and obviously cheerful and contented. Like all mountaineers, they are to the last degree hard-working. From early dawn until the last ray of daylight every one seems to be at work. The commune includes a number of small villages or hamlets of a few houses each, scattered about among the hills, many of them high up at the end of steep, rough roads hardly passable for the smallest vehicles. The farm-houses of which these hamlets are made up are large and evidently populous, and the barns are often detached. Already, early in September, with many of the crops still to be harvested, they seemed full to overflowing.

The whole country, at least wherever I traversed it, is covered with a thick peaty soil, which holds water like a sponge. In many places even grain in sheaves is not cured on the ground, but hung upon the forks of poles cut with the branches projecting, and standing in rows at the edges of the fields. Large crops are grown of what in England is called the horse-bean—tall-growing stalks, with pods along their sides. Even these cannot be cured on the ground; they are tied in bundles, which are hung in pairs over long poles, racks of which, twenty or thirty feet high and equally long, are an accompaniment of every barn, sometimes standing independently, supported by high poles, and sometimes resting on brackets built out from the front of the structure. Much of the land is so steep that I found difficulty in crossing it. From such fields the crops are removed in coarse linen sheets, making huge bundles, which are carried home on the heads of the people.

As many women as men are seen at work in the fields, and they do all manner of work equally, save that the ploughing and mowing are more often done by men, and the hoeing and reaping by women.

The frugality of their lives is equal to their industry; and with a fertile soil and a ready market, it is easy to understand the substantial prosperity which, for people of their class, is everywhere conspicuous. Their methods of life and work differ greatly from our own; their implements are rude and clumsy; their cattle are poor, cows being generally worked in the yoke; and it is easy to see many ways in which our example might be followed with great advantage. With a predilection, however, for village life for an agricultural people, I believe that, making allowance for their inferior education, the people in the villages about Cortina are more cheerful and contented than those of the corresponding class with us.

I have already referred to the accidents which occasionally befall workers upon the very steep mountain-sides of Tyrol. A very sad one occurred upon the day of our arrival at Cortina. A mother and her daughter and a young man were working in a hay-field which sloped steeply down to the edge of a precipice five or six hundred feet high. The mother slipped, but was arrested by a slight obstruction; the young man succeeded in reaching her, and might have saved her, but the child, becoming excited, hastened to them, fell, and carried them both with her over the fatal brink.

The approaches to the Ampezzo Valley from the north and west are over high passes, or through narrow defiles of the wildest and most rugged character, so that on arriving at Cortina from either direction one does not at first realize the splendor of its surroundings.

The enclosing mountains are in such harmony in their grandeur, the valley itself is so smiling and peaceful, and the town is so distant from the immediate hill-tops, that the views are less striking than at Campitello or Caprile. Gilbert and Churchill, on the occasion of their first visit, passed but a single night here, and only recognized after they had left, the fact that they had passed unnoticed the grandest combination of the dolomite peaks. So far as one could judge from simple appearance, the base of Monte Tofana was not half a mile from our windows. It is really more than two miles away, with a sturdy mountain and a deep valley intervening. A man on its summit cannot be seen with a strong field-glass. A long walk toward it soon tells the tale of its distance, and the distance reveals its stupendous height. Still farther away are the Cinque Torre and the Croda del Lago; and Antelao, which seems almost to peer over our shoulders, is ten miles distant. Every excursion that one makes and every different view obtained widens and lifts the horizon, until, after a few days' acquaintance, the surroundings of Cortina impress the imagination as does no other part of the dolomite region.

The social traveller will find his best entertainment, especially for a short stay, at one of the hotels in the town; but one "whose habits are studious and lonely" might prefer the pretty little bath-house (Ghedina's) nestled away among the trees at the mouth of a mountain valley two miles from Cortina. Its lower story is a little Italian grist-mill, whose rumbling wheels and stones and whose foaming brook sing a constant soothing lullaby. The upper story, with generous bath-rooms, tidy sleeping-rooms, and shaded galleries under

MONTE ANTELAO.

the broad roof, is little frequented by strangers, and the dense woods and steep hills are close at hand. The younger Ghedina's ready pencil has been busy all over the house, inside and out. It is from the neighborhood of this house that the best view is obtained of Monte Antelao, the highest mountain in sight from the Ampezzo Valley, and second only to the Marmolata. In the foreground is a little Alpine village, with its board-roofed crucifix.

"Over the hills and far away" to the south-west, in the valley of rich and beautiful Cordevole, lies the Italian village of Caprile, less comfortable and attractive than Cortina, but a capital centre for many excursions. Its dominant mountain is the Civita. Near it is the new-formed lake of Alleghe, created only in 1771 by the tumbling in of a great corner of Monte Pezza, burying two entire villages in the dead of night, and drowning two others in the suddenly dammed flood of the river. A few months later another slide falling into the lake drove great waves far up the shore, and worked even more destruction to property, if not to life. Where formerly all was activity and fertility and industry and frugal domestic happiness there is now only a sea of placid water, breathing no whisper of the vast calamity—a beautiful mountain lake, delighting the eye with the images of the smiling fields and dark woods and gray peaks in whose lap it lies. Like the Bergfall of the Taufers Thal only a few weeks since, and the great land-slide of Santa Croce centuries ago, the formation of Lake Alleghe instances the hazard attending the life and industry of these high-walled valleys.

One of the most serious drawbacks of travel lies in the need of leaving, perhaps forever, the new-found charms of so many halting-places. To pass all September and the early weeks of October among the dolomite Alps seemed far more attractive than the further wandering and the rough voyage to which we were destined; but the destiny was fixed, and we must leave Cortina. Happily our smooth road-way led ever on among these glorious mountains, and Cadore, with its beauty and its associations, lacked nothing of the interest, nor, in its way, of the charm, of the higher valleys we had left.

Mrs. Edwards says: "For myself, looking back in memory across

CIVITA AND LAKE ALLEGHE.

that intervening sea of peaks and passes which lies between Bozen and Cortina, I am inclined to place the Ampezzo Dolomites in the very first rank both as regards position and structure. The mountains of Primiero are more extravagantly wild in outline, the Marmolata carries more ice and snow, the Civita is more beautiful, the solitary giants of the Seisser Alp are more imposing;

but taken as a group, I know nothing, whether for size, variety, or picturesqueness, to equal that great circle which, within a radius of less than twelve miles from the doors of the Aquila Nera, includes the Pelmo, Antelao, Marmarole, Croda Malcora, Cristallo, and Tofana."

My own retrospection of a much more limited experience confirms Mrs. Edwards's judgment. Comparing Cortina not only with other dolomite regions, but with all the crowd of charming and beautiful corners of Tyrol, and with the grandest of its other mountains, it seems to me *facile princeps*. Neither have I found elsewhere such a combination of qualities which invite to a longer acquaintance.

CHAPTER XIV.

THE ASCENT OF MONTE TOFANA.

I HAD had serious misgivings since writing as I did about peak-climbing. It was obviously presumptuous in one who had only made the ascent of Mount Washington—in an omnibus—to question a practice which has so many intelligent devotees. The gentle climb to the Coll di Rondella, and its charming uplook to the great dolomite peaks, had added to my apprehension that I had overstepped the limits of good judgment, if not of good taste; for surely, if this moderate elevation could so magnify the grandeur of the surrounding mountains, it seemed possible that a still higher position might increase the effect in like proportion. If so, then mountain-climbing must be its own exceeding great reward.

It was no easy matter to convince myself of the prudence of undertaking a task of such notorious difficulty. With limbs untrained to up-hill work, with lungs gauged by long residence to the sea-level scale, with more pounds avoirdupois than any "Bergführer" or Alpine Club man that I had seen in Tyrol, and with no consuming ambition for the cragsman's exploits, the weight of the argument would have been strongly against the attempt, but for that unfortunate paragraph, which made it a matter of honor for me to try what I had questioned, and to make open confession if the event should prove me wrong. The conviction came slowly but surely that, despite all drawbacks, I must at least make an earnest attempt to get to the top of a high mountain.

The beautiful *pergola* where I now write, opens north, east, and west upon one of the loveliest of valleys, a valley shut in by Cristallo, Antelao, Croda Malcora, Monte Pelmo, the Rochetta, the Becco di Mezzodi, Monte Gusella, Monte Nuvolau, and Monte Tofana, the noblest

CINQUE TORRE AND NUVALAU.

group of Tyrolean peaks. The triple head of Monte Tofana challenges the carrying out of my growing resolution. Seven of the surrounding mountains named above are over 10,000 feet high (Antelao, 10,890). The middle peak of Tofana is 10,724 feet above the sea.

Ball says that its ascent is "for the practised mountaineer one of the most attractive expeditions to be made in this district." Baedekker says, "The ascent of the higher mountains requires experience; that which best repays the fatigue is Monte Tofana." Amthor calls it "schwer." On the whole, it seemed that, should I succeed in making this ascent, I should have done my whole duty, and the decision was definitely fixed. Late one night, when the bright starlight following a week of beautiful September weather gave good promise for the morrow, I sent for Ginseppe Ghedina, who had been recommended by a friend as a skilful and *judicious* guide, and arranged for the expedition. Diligent Filomena, of the Aquila Nera, undertook the preparation of supplies with an air which savored the least in the world of doubt as to the result of my effort. I asked the landlord whether there was any difficulty about my making the ascent, and he asked whether I had ever made a "Bergpartie" before. My negative answer was met with an involuntary shrug of the shoulders, and brought no other reply. The guide said that I could at least go a part of the way. With these doubtful assurances, I went early and not altogether confidently to bed.

We were to start at half-past three, and I was called at three. By way of economizing my untried forces, I had engaged a mule for the first two hours and a half; and here a saddle-mule implies a man to lead it. I had provided myself overnight with a sturdy glass of milk, with a dash of Cayenne pepper, to begin the day. In the kitchen of the hotel I found the cook well advanced with her day's work, coffee and hot milk ready, and Kaisersemmeln freshened in the oven—so the usual Tyrolean breakfast was added to the milk. Then came a delay about eggs. Giuseppe could not find them among the abundant provender. He advised waiting until a supply of ten could be boiled. These being ready, it was found that Filomena had already furnished four—a number which he regarded as entirely insignificant. In his search he had mistaken them for a package of salt. All being ready, he slung his "Rucksack" containing the food and two bottles of wine. On top of this was strapped an ominous coil of half-inch rope some fifty feet long, and three pairs of heavy sharp-pointed iron crampons, the whole weighing about twenty pounds. Over his shoulder he carried a short iron-pointed alpenstock, with an ice-pick at its upper end. A second alpenstock was carried by the mule-leader.

We set out at four o'clock. It was still quite dark, no gleam of dawn appearing in the sky, which, studded with stars, was only less black than the high mountains whose serrated edges were cut in sharp silhouette against it. Two black pedestrians and one black man on a black mule were hardly distinguishable between the black house fronts along the main street of Cortina. The stars shone brightly over the gray roadway, and far away to the south, over the crest of the Croda Malcora, Jupiter twinkled with weird green light. We were soon climbing a country road, past farm-houses and barns and running fountains, through fields studded with rows of wheat-sheaves or redolent with the odor of half-cured hay. As we crept up the side of the valley the great gleam of the morning-star came suddenly over the sharp mountain-top, big and brilliant, like a fire-balloon just launched from the crest of Sorapis.

Little by little the gray dawn, which had already lighted the summit of Tofana, touched one after another the edges of the crags, and poured slowly over into the valley, picking out its whitened house fronts, and gradually defining the breaks and gorges in its rocks. Star after star faded from view, until Venus alone was left shining over the hills. Lights sparkled here and there from the scattered houses, the varied hum of awakening day came up from the valley, and the whole hill-side was filled with the music of tinkling bells as the cattle and sheep roused to their morning grass. The steady droning flow of gossip between my Italian attendants suggested no ideas to interrupt my morning reverie, and my thoughts naturally turned to the expedition on which I was bent. The outlook was entirely changed.

Under the stimulus and excitement of the early start, and the charm of unfamiliar daybreak, I came to take a new view of mountaineering. I could well imagine that no occupation of a manly life, save fox-hunting alone, could offer so much of what a vigorous and sound-bodied man should enjoy. Climbing slowly and steadily up the steep bridle-path toward a peak which only the sturdiest and most patient effort could reach, I felt for the moment how puerile had been my earlier conceptions, and I was ready to enroll myself as a permanent member of the stalwart band of Alpine climbers.

Two hours and a half brought us to the foot of the steep mass of débris which filled the gorge of the mountain to a height of over three thousand feet above us. It was now broad day, but the gorge was shaded from the morning sun. The mule and leader were dismissed, my poncho was strapped to Ghedina's rucksack, I took the alpenstock, and we started stoutly up the steep mass of large stones which had rolled down over the gravel, and piled themselves up as a buttress against it. This passed, we struck the finer drift — a loose mass of stones, precisely such as are used for macadamizing roads, angular and sharp, but with a remarkable facility of movement. Indeed, it has adjusted itself at the angle where its movement ceases, and it needs only the slightest impulse to set it moving again, so that each step up was followed by a downward slip, and the miles of advance needed to take us over that single mile of our way can be measured only by the strained muscles and the deep and quickened breath they entailed.

Here, as throughout the whole ascent, the view was by no means what one would imagine. One's eyes were bent alone upon the next spot where foothold must be found. At constantly shortening intervals, as the toil accumulated, and as the air grew lighter, it became necessary to halt and sit, pant and take breath. Two hours of hard, monotonous, weary, breathless toil took us to a point, still far below the top of the slide, where foothold could be gained, on a narrow ledge of sharp rocks running up at its side.

It was curious to notice how, during the course of this task—the hardest labor (not compulsory) that man can undertake—the enthusiasm which had overtaken me while in the saddle had oozed away. It gradually gave place to a conviction that he who would thus apply the severest physical effort of which his nature is capable must be actuated by some higher and stronger motive than I had in my wildest anticipations connected with the achievement I had attempted. But for that instinct which leads us not to turn back when once the plough is set in its furrow, I fear that I might have abandoned the project, and left the top of Tofana food for my imagination alone. But the motive which impels us to pursue to the bitter end a self-imposed task prevailed.

We had started up the drift at half-past six, and it was now nearly nine. Two hours more would bring us to the top.

I now learned the use of the rope. One of its ends was tied securely round my waist, the other forming a noose over Ghedina's shoulder. The primary object was for security against a fall, most of the length being coiled and held in the guide's hand. But as my knees grew weak, and as my breath grew short almost to gasping, then I would sit on the sharp edge of the fractured cliff, brace myself with the alpenstock against some crevice below, clutch with the other hand a sharp corner of stone above, and wait until Ghedina had paid out the whole length of the rope, and fixed himself in some secure position above me. Then he would gradually toll me up with a steady and friendly pull, cautioning me how to step, how to plant my prod, and how to test the crackled rock before I trusted myself to hold by it. A wonderful help was that rope—a moral and yet a physical help too. It showed how nearly I had come to the end of my force that so slight an added impulse should make such vast difference in my progress and in the husbanding of my wind. The regular intermitting of the work, too, and the considerable pauses, were a great help. The progress was not less, and the ease was much greater. No, not ease. Heaven forbid that I should use that word anywhere in this connection! I mean simply that the actual muscular, synovial, cardiac, and pulmonary suffering was abated.

A hard half-hour of this "ride-and-tie" business brought us to the first low crest, or *Joch*, between two peaks. Here, so far as I was able to divert my attention from the various unusual manifestations of my own person—ears crackling, limbs trembling, mouth parched, every vein throbbing, and every pore perspiring—I became conscious of the most majestic surroundings. Not only the Val Travernenze, which opened amidst the wildest turmoil of distorted mountain-sides before us, and the enormous glacier which fills the vast hollowed slope of the Marmolata, but almost equally the immediate mountain-sides behind us, under which we had crept, intent only upon the ground beneath our feet, would, observed in a serener mood, justify one's highest imagination of mountain wildness and grandeur. They impress me more in recollection than they did in the actual but disturbed observation.

No time could be spared for sights by the way-side, however imposing, and we pressed on, now on a narrow ledge at the side of a precipice at what would have been a giddy height had the attention not been fixed upon foot-hold and hand-hold at every step. Indeed, it seems to me that herein lies the safety of the mountain climber's work. He must be unconscious of all that is above and of all that is below him, holding his attention closely to his immediate surroundings, so that the sense of elevation is lost. We came out later upon a crest from which there was a vast slope of débris reaching down to the edge of a precipice far below, and stretching on before us to the wide and steep glacier which fills the northern slope below the twin peaks. Here came the most disheartening part of the trip. After all our toilsome and weary struggle upward, it seemed more than discouraging to have to go six or eight hundred feet lower down to reach the foot of the glacier, from which point only we could make the final ascent. Fortunately the débris was tolerably firm, and in spite of the precipice to which it led, the passage was not especially dangerous. The emotions with which I looked back up our steep oblique track, and thought of the return, were anything but cheering.

At the end of this part of the route lay a patch of hard snow some twenty feet wide, in which the guide had to chop footholds as we progressed. The glacier is in shape like a section of a funnel, thirty feet wide at the base, six or eight hundred feet wide at the top, and perhaps a thousand feet high. It is quite regularly curved laterally, is crossed by several crevasses of little width, and is spotted with stones which have rolled on to it from the rocks above. We drank copiously of the cold stream which flows out below it, and about which the rocks were all covered with a thin film of ice. Crossing the stream, and climbing up the far side of the gorge through which it runs, we halted to adjust the crampons. These are stout iron frames reaching from the middle of the heel to the ball of the foot, with a sharp spike three-quarters of an inch long at each corner, and with a stout loop turned up at each side of the foot. Through these loops a strap is passed, and this is bound over the instep, in my case with the utmost strength of Ghedina's wiry fingers and strong teeth. Those of my readers who skated in the old days of rude strapping will understand the energy with which I protested against the severity of his work. But he insisted that absolute tightness was essential to safety, and I accepted this further infliction of pain with trained submission.

We now began the steep ascent of the glacier, the process being to strike the point of the alpenstock into a firm hold, then to advance one foot and make sure that its crampon was fast fixed in the ice, then to advance the alpenstock again, and then the other foot. This continued for twenty minutes, with an occasional halt for breath, and with a constant wounding of the feet by the tightly bound straps. In spite of the tightness, one of my irons came loose, and we had to stop in mid-ice to readjust it, this time without regard to protests. I had listened with curious interest to the jingling of those irons throughout the morning. I had inspected their long sharp points, and had looked forward with some impatience to the moment when they should be added to my experiences. I have not often felt such real pleasure as I did when we came again upon the hard rock, and they were removed. I will not say that when Ghedina tucked them away under a stone by the path-side, I hoped that he would not be able to find them again; but even their loss would not have been entirely without compensation.

Such pleasure and elation as I felt from treading again upon *terra firma* soon yielded as the further climbing began. It is not worth while to describe it. It only lasted about forty minutes, panting spells included, and much of my upward course was steadied, if not assisted, by the kindly tension of the stout arm at the other end of the rope.

At last we came to a point where the strata of the mountain are crumbled by the sharp angle at which they were bent. It is as though the finger-point of a Titan had been pressed up under the stiff leaves of this great volume of geologic history, raising them to a peak and cracking them at the bend.

The air had become very light, and the breathing induced by such exertion grew painful. Three thousand feet below, the nostrils had become too small, and the open mouth had to help to pump in the needed supply. Lips, tongue, palate, and throat were parched and tired. We halted only fifty feet below the peak. Had it been a hundred feet, i' faith I fear I should have failed to reach it; at fifty feet I did reach it—the absolute top. Ghedina began to discourse upon the many distant peaks within sight. I begged him to wait. The air was perfectly clear, and not at all cold, the breeze only fresh. Being warm and exhausted, I threw the poncho over my shoulders, took the coiled rope for an arm rest, and stretched out over a sloping couch of precisely the composition one sees in a stone-breaker's half-finished heap at the roadside. I have had few so restful half-hours as that passed on this unsybaritic bed. Ghedina gave me a tumbler of wine. I drank a single swallow, took the glass from my lips, looked in vague and half-unconscious wonder over the billowy clouds resting in a sheltered valley below, and was startled from my sleep by spilling the wine over my other hand. That was all—probably not fifteen seconds—but it gave the mysterious change which comes only with absolute sleep. The blood coursed with a quieter impulse; the eye became steadier, and the brain clearer. I was able to give attention to the details of all that one sees from a mountain-top.

The long road of the Ampezzo Valley looked like narrow bobbin trailed over the dark green fields and among the specks of houses. Cortina, three miles and a half distant by the line of sight, looked, through the clear air, like a toy village out of a wooden box. We fancied that with the strong glass we saw a man in its streets. The bell calling the people to mid-day mass rang clear in our ears.

Except for this little stretch of inhabited valley, all else was an unmeaning mass of distorted rock, desolate, cruel, Dantesque, incoherent chaos, without expression, without interest, and without charm. The great peaks of Eastern Switzerland, the sharp point of the Oertler, the Oetzthal group, the Stubaier Ferner, the Grosser Venediger, the Gross Glockner, and the peaks of the Carinthian and Illyrian Alps, stretching over more than two hundred miles of the horizon from west to east, were all in clear view, all near, and *all low*. Their height barely brought them into the plane of vision. They and the great ice-field of the Marmolata all seemed lower than Tofana itself. And Tofana had lost its majesty. Seen from below, it was sublime. Conquered by the toiling tread of two insignificant men, it became mere stone beneath our feet.

We stayed at the summit an hour and a half, I wrapped in extra clothing, the hardy Ghedina with his coat off and his breast bare, as unconcerned as though he had only mowed his swath through a hayfield. Inserted in a crevice of the rock is a wide-mouthed bottle, corked with a stone, containing a roll of papers bearing the names of those who have made the ascent. It is uninteresting to those who have added their own names to the list, and unknown to the rest of the world.

The descent, at first easy, soon involved the previous trials taken in the inverse direction. Going down the glacier, the crampons hurt differently, but they hurt equally. Climbing from the foot of the glacier to the crest of the lower pass called for a renewed exercise of a strength that was already worn and overtaxed.

From near this pass the descent is directly down the slide, a steep and endless incline of sharp road metal. At first it is novel and interesting, this quick descent. The angular gravel lies on a pitch at which its movement barely stops. Set in motion again by any cause, it slips and rattles and rolls as though it would go to the very bottom of the valley. Standing upon it and bearing heavily backward against the alpenstock whose point is buried in it, a slight movement of the feet sets the mass rolling. Faster and faster it goes, deeper and deeper sink the feet, until the very mountain-side moves like a stream of broken stone and carries us along with it. When the feet are buried more than ankle-deep, when the shoes are filled with sharp pebbles, and when the speed becomes too great for safety, we step aside and stand until the avalanche is stilled, and then begin a new movement on a fresh course. Occasionally we come upon an accumulation of larger and firmer stones, over which it is necessary to walk. After endurance had ceased to be a virtue, I would take off my shoes and pour out the accumulated geological specimens which had made even resting a penance. By the time we had reached the point where the mule had been left—now about two o'clock—I was convinced that the only reason why the coming down a mountain is not so bad as the going up is that it takes less time.

Here, sitting under the shade of the first fir-trees, and somewhat suffused with the satisfaction that comes of the finishing of a serious task, I was able to regard this face of Tofana in a friendly spirit. Viewed as mere rock-work, the steep-walled sides of this the entrance hall, and the majestic crest beyond it, are probably unsurpassed by anything that Nature has done in her sternest stone-building mood. There is nothing fantastic, but there is a grandeur and solidity and directness of purpose which seemed to me to ally this great pile of rectangular strata more closely with the work of the pigmy architects than any other rocks of this region. If I might offer a word of guidance to those who are led to visit this mountain, especially those who have seen its opposite side from the Coll di Rondella, it would be to come here to this foot of the great avalanche of stone, to this last reach of the hardy fir, and fill the soul and the memory full with the stupendous masses and the marvellous colors of these great bastions; to contemplate from below, and from below only, that rising stretch of desolate, helpless, impending débris, and the noble crags which tower above it, and then, unwearied and not disenchanted, to go back over the well-grown slope and through the sunny fields to cheery Cortina.

Of my further descent I will only say that all the miles of down-hill walking, added to the down-hill climbing, made by far the severest strain upon the hold-back part of my harness to which it was ever subjected. I hailed with pleasure the steep little hill which rises from the bridge over the Boita to the main street of the village.

At five o'clock I sat down to beer and tranquil tobacco and entire rest. The questions and the interest of friends kept me from sleeping, and little by little the more acute sensations subsided in my joints. Later, food and a long night's sleep, and, above all, the pure and invigorating air of this enchanted valley, restored me to the condition of a sore and stiffened but a rested and cheerful being.

I would not give up my recollection of this ascent for the price of a first-rate hunter, but I would not make it again for the finest horse that ever followed hounds.

CHAPTER XV.

TO THE MESURINA ALP.

The best-rewarded excursion that I made was eastward over the Tre Croce Pass, a high saddle between the Croda Malcora and Monte Cristallo, two thousand feet higher than Cortina. Here is a little hospice for the shelter of storm-overtaken travellers—a rude stone hut, with a hearth and chimney in one corner. Though the day was warm, I could not resist the temptation to gratify a passion inherited from boyhood, and build a roaring fire with the dried pine boughs with which the floor was strewn.

Mistaking the directions of the guide-book, I made a needless steep ascent and immediate descent of an extra thousand feet, being rewarded, however, with a rich harvest of wild flowers, with which the little alp at the summit is studded in great variety.

In many excursions and along many roadsides we were constantly struck with the rich masses of September flowers, and especially with the great preponderance of every shade of blue. The greenish-gray Edelweiss and the red Alpen Rosen are the typical Alpine flowers, but we found their blue sisters in far greater abundance, among them many varieties of gentian, but none so beautiful as our own fringed one.

Another hour's hard tramp brought me to the Mesurina Alp, a vast open pasture surrounded by fir woods, and these by the great mountain-peaks, stretching down at its northern end to the pretty little Mesurina Lake. Two hundred and fifty cows were jingling their bells and feeding over its short green grass. They were a very pretty and picturesque herd, almost universally of a solid gray color, with black muzzles and switches. Could they be baptized as Jerseys and sent to England, their color would make their fortune. They had little else to recommend them. Like all the cows of this region, and of Tyrol generally, they are thin, without the evidence of great milking to justify their thinness. A good udder is rarely seen, or, in fact, a good cow. At the upper side of the pasture an enormous octagonal shed, the outer

MISURINA LAKE AND THE DREI ZINNEN.

wall of which is of stone masonry and very high, furnishes shelter for this entire herd, and encloses an open yard where all may lie comfortably in the sun.

The chalet of the establishment is a large, low, rambling, dingy stone house, given over mainly to buttery and cheese-room. At one corner a low-walled room about twelve by eighteen feet, running up into a high roof, is the living-room of the cow-herds and dairy-men. A broad low shelf surrounding the room serves as a seat by day and as a couch at night. In the middle of the floor, on the rough stone hearth, a wood fire boils a large kettle in which the *polenta* (hasty-pudding)—the sole food of these men, except skimmed milk—is cooked. The open door and one very small unglazed window furnish the only entrance for light and air and the only exit for smoke, the rafters and shingles of the roof being black as coal. They gave me a two-quart kettle of milk to drink, and entertained themselves with an interested criticism of my dress, but this in low-voiced Italian, lest it should give offence. I gave twenty kreutzers (less than nine cents) for my entertainment, which boundless liberality opened their hearts, and they took me over the whole dingy establishment. By far the larger part of the house is occupied by the drying-room, where several tons of Schweitzer and Parmesan cheese were spread out upon shelves. The cheese was good, but the butter, of which at least half a ton was on hand awaiting shipment, was anything but inviting.

Should any of my readers happen to have a moderate capital, agricultural tastes, and delicate lungs, I commend to his attention the exploitation of this high-lying and beautiful alp, sheltered on all sides by great dolomite mountains.

A mile beyond the chalet, at the edge of the lake, stands a little Italian inn, well known to travellers among these hills for its stock of capital Asti wine, its hard gray bread, and wholesome cheese — and nothing else save dirt and smoke and dismal discomfort. However, with such a lake as the Mesurina, and such peaks as Monte Piano and the Drei Zinnen, and such a great fringe of fir and weird mountain-top, and such wine as Asti, the pedestrian may well be content.

Following the shorter direct road, I came into Cortina at dusk, literally unfatigued, after a walk of twenty-seven miles, including a climb of three thousand feet, and much steep up-and-down work among the foot-hills. This, be it understood, was on the second day after climbing Tofana. It indicated better than anything else could the great value of the air of these mountains as a help to bodily exercise; for I am not a practised walker, being rarely afoot an hour out of the twenty-four. Delicate persons with whom we conversed say that here, in the absence of oppressive heat, and in the exhilarating atmosphere, they find themselves tempted to constant exercise, and vastly benefited by it. Being of sound body, I cannot myself speak from the invalid point of view, but I found myself constantly stimulated for severe work which at home I should shun even in the finest weather.

Before taking leave of the Dolomites it may be useful to refer to the theories concerning their formation, still a moot question among geologists. The weight of the argument seems to favor the conclusion of Baron Richthofen, that they are the work of coral insects, formed upon the lower rocks at the bed of a deep salt sea, and raised by slow upheaval to their present elevation. He bases his hypothesis upon the correspondence of their forms and their surroundings with what is known concerning the coral reefs of the Pacific, the isolation of their masses from other corresponding formations, the improbability of their peculiar shapes being due to meteoric denudation, the undisturbed beds beneath them and occasionally above them, and the very unequal thickness of the deposit at different points—an inequality in which it would seem that the other rocks in their neighborhood would have shared had it been due to erosive or atmospheric action.

CHAPTER XVI.

FROM THE GREAT PEAKS TO THE LAGUNES.

WE were sleeping at the very Italian Albergo di Cadore, at Tai, ten minutes' walk from Pieve di Cadore, higher up in the hills. There, in a dingy little stone house, now occupied by uncleanly peasants, its floors begrimed with dirt and its ceilings blackened with smoke, the great Venetian, Tiziano Vecellio, four hundred years ago entered upon his illustrious life. The outer wall bears the inscription:

NEL MCCCCLXXVII
FRA QUESTE VMILI MURA
TIZIANO VECELLIO
VENE A CELEBRE VITA
DONDE VSCOVA GIA PRESSO A CENTO ANNO
IN VENEZIA
ADDI XXVII AGOSTO
MDLXXVI

A longer life of industrious labor has not been led in modern times, and the world is still glorious with his work.

We were roused before the first gleam of day. Over the black, fir-clad hills peered the weird moon-lit peaks of the Antelao, Marmarole, Pelmo, and Civita. Against the dark woods the face of the campanile and the scattered house fronts stood white and clear. The river rolled far below us through a dark mysterious cleft, toward which wound the white Ampezzo road.

By the time that the gray light of morning had filled the sky, and thrown the morn-light into shadow and bathed the mountain-tops in a rosy glow, we were comfortably packed away in our little Einspänner and rolling out of the town. In our day's drive we were to descend nearly three thousand feet. The mountains were high and steep, and the valleys were deep and dark. The road now clung to the hill-sides, now crossed high arches of fine masonry, now zigzagged back and forth down the hill-side, or drove far up into a valley—always descending, but always gently—always winding, and always protected at its outer side by mason-work. It often showed as a broad white band far below us, and often as a terrace borne upon strong arches above us. At every step and at every turn it brought into view new beauties and new marvels of these wonderful Dolomite walls.

Through all this majesty, through the many stone-built and smoke-blackened villages, among the cheerful, graceful, much-soiled, and happy Italian people, the attention is always interested, but never more than by this great Austro-Italian highway itself, over which we roll as over a floor. It must have been more costly than any railroad, and its maintenance in its universally good condition must be a serious matter. A railroad gets over many natural difficulties by tunnelling, and this gives it a greater command over its grades. On a carriage road long tunnels are not admissible, and the grade has to be taken on such ground as offers itself. The Brenner road presented many engineering obstacles, and is a masterly work; but the more sudden angles and deeper valleys of the Dolomite country offer greater difficulties, and this work, from Toblach to Conegliano, impressed me as the most interesting of its class that I have seen. It has the fault so common in public roads of being too wide, generally about twenty-five feet. The used portion—that which seems to contain all the wheel tracks, including turning out—is rarely more than fifteen feet, and it need never be more. The remaining ten feet have to be kept free from weeds by hoeing. In many places fully ten feet of the width on one side or the other is occupied with heaps of road metal, proving that the remaining space is sufficient. It would, of course, have been cheaper in construction and maintenance to make a road fifteen feet wide with occasional bays for stone-breaking.

The Piave, down whose valley our course lay, is a very considerable stream, winding through a broad bed of desolate gray stone brought down by the floods, a dismal setting for its beryl-colored waters. It passes many villages built of the stone against whose solid masses they cling. Little fertile land is to be seen, and one wonders how the population, even with its obvious severe labor, subsists. The lumber-driving and the frequent saw-mills employ many men, and the constant rectification of the course of the river and the maintenance of the frequent shoots through which the logs are driven occupy many women with most arduous stone-carrying—in baskets at their backs. Despite their hard life, they seem cheerful and careless and happy. The children gathering manure on the highway, and the women, with their busy distaffs, at the doorways, showed little evidence of absolute

"THE WOMEN WITH THEIR BUSY DISTAFFS."

poverty. Of beggars we saw very few. The children who followed the carriage, calling for kreutzers, begged from inclination rather than from necessity.

Longarone, a large, dull town, where we breakfasted, had its streets filled with stands of beautiful fruit; but the land about it seemed barren, and the reason for its being was not obvious. We were still in the midst of dolomite mountains, but no longer among the great peaks.

The characteristic forms of the hill-tops could still be traced, but they had come down beneath the extreme limit of vegetation, and were modified by the growth of trees, and by the more frequent action of freezing and thawing.

Later, near Belluno, we left the swift-flowing Piave, and followed its long-abandoned original course through a valley which a great land-slip, possibly in prehistoric times, dammed to a height of six hundred feet, forcing the river to find exit through another gap in the mountains, and turning a part of its old bed into the broad bright blue lake of Santa Croce. The old lower valley of the Piave is fed with only the mountain rills which were formerly its insignificant branches. Here begins the little brook which, filling the basins of a series of little lakes, grows to a respectable stream by the time it leaves the hills at Serravalle, irrigates the rich meadows of Venetia, and pours into the Adriatic far to the east of the new mouth of the Piave.

At the summit of the broad dam stands Fadalto—a few houses and the little inn where we dined. It is a memorable inn, tidy in its appointments, and though thoroughly Italian, very passable as to its table. Its kitchen was the most picturesque and the prettiest that we had anywhere seen—a long room with tables for the commoner guests, with huge whitewashed beams hung with shining utensils of embossed copper, with a latticed screen, behind which the handsome and smiling and cleanly padrona herself prepared the food. It would have been a noticeable room without the great bay containing the huge hearth of the country, which was its chief feature. This hearth is a white marble pedestal about twenty inches high and seven feet square, with its corners cut away. Its centre is of brick. On this burns a wood fire open on all sides. Above, a funnel of wood painted black, and as large as the hearth, gathers the smoke to the chimney. From its border there hangs a woollen curtain eight inches wide. The sides of the bay under the windows are furnished with a broad high seat, to which the edges of the hearth serve as a footstool; under this are the wood-boxes. Enormous polished iron andirons and numerous copper vessels stand upon the hearth, a great black soup-kettle hanging from its chain completing the picture. A cosier nook for winter evening gossip could not be desired.

FIREPLACE IN ITALIAN INN AT FADALTO.

Our journey, which had begun at six, led us on through the lowering hills, and finally out on to the fertile plain of Venetia, where the twin towns of Serravalle and Cenada, with their well-planted connecting *allée* and spacious half-way theatre and casino, brought us suddenly into an atmosphere all Italian, and where already our Tyrol Einspänner was regarded with curious interest.

At half-past eight Jane and I were in a gondola, under the light of the full harvest-moon and a cloudless sky and breathless air, floating down the Grand Canal.

CHAPTER XVII.

A MORNING IN THE STREETS OF VENICE.

We first touched the shore of modern civilization at Venice—a shore washed by the waters of antiquity and of quaint provincialism, and strewn with the flotsam and jetsam of all times and of many strange peoples. It is an entirely new land to one who comes from the haunts of the simple Tyrolese.

My rustic pen must refrain from a description of this sweet city of the sea. Where so many of the world's best artists have laid their smoothest verse and their most graceful periods in homage, no word of mine need seek a place. To the solemn, spell-bound spirit-city of the past I offer only the tribute of silent love and admiration. Its crumbling balconies and its slime-grown and water-lapped thresholds, the mellow glow of its over-ripe façades, and the soft shimmer of its color-fed lagunes, will attract and enchant the beauty-loving world without my help.

One of its aspects, however, seems to me to have received inadequate notice. Wreathed within the city of the canals and the gondolas, co-extensive with it, and growing from the same core of humanity, lies unobserved the quiet and hidden city of the streets—a city full of strange people, busy with the indolence and unthrift of Italian daily life.

Hoping to catch the first movement of the day, I went out at half-past six. In France it should have been quite two hours earlier, but here I struck the very beginning of the morning life. A sleepy and uncombed waiter was giving coffee to a few straggling guests on the Riva, drowsy fishermen were just hoisting their painted sails, and one after another the gondoliers of the Piazzetta were creeping from under their awnings and stretching their languid arms in regret for the ended night. About the steps of the Campanile, and in every sheltered corner, beggars were still dreaming on the pavement. The Piazza was piled here and there with the chairs and tables at which last night delegates from all nations had sat under the moonlight, sipping coffee and ices, and drinking in the mellow glory of the golden mosaic portals of San Marco. The pigeons, lineal descendants of Dandolo's carriers, were picking the last crumbs from the clean pavement, and broad day filled the whole deserted square.

Turning the corner of the church, and crossing the canal which passes under the Bridge of Sighs, I left the Venice of the gondola, and penetrated a labyrinth of narrow streets—footways only, for no hoof ever awakens their echoes—which led in and out among the houses and garden-walls; up and down over narrow bridges; into little squares where fruit-women were setting up their stands, and where seedy men were taking morning cocktails of black coffee and brandy at the tables in front of the caffè; to the doors of grand churches where matutinal women were attending mass; and into many a cul-de-sac whence the steps must be retraced.

I met respectable middle-aged clerks, in well-worn black, who bought their morning papers and trudged on to their desks—men who had come out from their own homes, and were going to their regular bread-winning work, whose round of life lies in this strange place, and whose familiar daily scenes are those marvels which we come so far to see—men to whom the name America brings only vague suggestions of New York and Brazil. I think this impresses me more than anything else. To have a foreigner in the streets turn and look at me as though not he but I myself were the interesting object—this is the most unsettling sight of all my seeings.

Little by little business began to take possession of the streets. Bakers' shops and butchers' shops and fish-stalls were opened; the din of countless blacksmiths and coppersmiths filled the air at every turn, as though the making of locks and kettles and chimney-pots were the one usurping industry of the world; loud-voiced women called all the people to come and partake of baked pumpkin, fresh and hot, and the melody of mingled street cries swelled to a chorus of supplication.

Lately risen maidens lowered baskets from their balconies, and fished up cat-meat, or bread, or onions, or other household supplies, lowered the coppers for payment, gathered their scanty raiment about

BALCONY MARKETING.

them, and withdrew. The vender—we knew him at the opera—pocketed his money, tossed his load to his head, and yelled his noisy way down the alley.

In the Piazza beyond the Rialto, where early activity most centres, I took up a commanding position at an out-of-door table, and ordered my "white coffee" and bread-and-butter. What a wonderful place it was for breakfasting—just for once! What pretty but carelessly powdered women, in black lace head-dresses, those were who came from each street and went toward the church; what a clatter the wooden pattens made, and what a gabble the newsboys; what loads of fresh fruit and vegetables the women carried past; how the urchins gambled for soldi; how unlike everything was to what we see at home; and how unreal one grew to feel himself in watching it all!

The cheap dealers of the Rialto were taking down their shutters as I crossed it, and displaying their low-priced wares. Boys sat on the broad steps munching bread and revelling in the yellow luxury of broad wedges of hot and savory pumpkin. The purveyors of the adjacent quarters were climbing the steps with whole head-loads of grapes, or fish, or vegetables. Over the hand-rail, filling the whole width of the Grand Canal, lay a fleet of barges unloading produce from beyond the lagunes, or stowing away assorted cargoes of white and purple grapes, peaches, figs, lettuce, chiccory, radishes, shining white onions, carrots, beets, potatoes—the whole fresh-colored assortment of green-grocery. On shore the market people filled the streets and the arcades with fish, and flesh, and fowl, and fruit, and flowers, and the whole air with a tumult of noisy traffic. I descended among the throng, where customers were being importuned on every hand, and where sharp bargains were being driven in sprats and snails and in fractions of the smallest fowl.

Entering a little square shut in by high houses, and, like most Venetian squares, dominated by the unfinished façade of a time-stained church, I noticed a singular activity among the people. They were scurrying in from every alley, and hastening from every house-door, with odd-shaped copper buckets on hook-ended wooden bows, and with little coils of rope. Old men and women, boys and girls, all gathered closely about a covered well-curb in the middle of the square; and still they hurried on, until they stood a dozen deep around it. Presently the church tower slowly struck eight, and a little old man forced his way through the crowd, passed his ponderous iron key through the lid, and unlocked the well. The kettles went jangling into it, and came slopping out again at an amazing rate, and the people trudged off home, each with a pair of them swung from the shoulder. The wells are deep cisterns, which are filled during the night, and it is out of amiable consideration for those who love their morning nap that they are given as good a chance as their neighbors of getting an unroiled sup-

AT THE PUBLIC WELL.—A MORNING SCENE IN VENICE.

ply. This is the first instance that has come to my notice of a commendable municipal restraint upon the reprehensible practice of early rising. Few, very few, of those who came for water had had time for their toilets. Their day evidently begins with this excursion to the public reservoir.

Later in my walk I saw a cistern being replenished. A barge filled with fresh-water lay in a canal near by, and a steam-pump forced the supply through a hose to the square, where a gutter carried it to the well. The water is of excellent quality. It is brought through conduits from the Enganean Hills, near Padua, but its distribution through the city is carried on in the original manner here indicated. For a city where the salt sea is the scavenger, where ablutions are not *de rigueur*, where fires cannot rage, and where water is not a beverage, the cost of laying distributing mains has wisely been spared.

By nine o'clock I had walked some miles, and had seen the populace subside from its brief spasm of activity and settle down to the sweet do-nothing of its daily life, and I turned my face homeward. I sought in vain for a ferry over the Grand Canal. I was lost in a maze of confusing streets. Defeated of my purpose, I called a gondola, and was rowed ignominiously back to my hotel.

CHAPTER XVIII.

CIRCUMLOCUTION.

From Botzen I had sent a trunk to Venice by freight-train, and I went to the station to get it. I was met by a porter who had served in the Austrian army, and who spoke German. He kindly took my case in hand. Armed with my receipt, I was conducted to a freight clerk's office. He looked through many pigeon-holes, and shrugged his shoulders—my trunk had not arrived. I expostulated. He looked again, and again shrugged. Fourteen days should have sufficed, but he had as yet received no notice of the arrival. My porter took me to the custom-house; there stood the trunk, covered with a week's dust. Back to the freight clerk; he looked again. No, the freight letter had not arrived. I did not want the letter, I wanted the trunk. He shrugged his shoulders; we must wait until the *chef* should come. At last the *chef* came. He remembered having seen the letter, and he looked through the pigeon-holes. He must be mistaken; it could not have come. No matter about the letter, my receipt was a duplicate, and I wanted the trunk. The *chef* shrugged his shoulders. Then he went off to rummage through a desk at another corner of the room, and at last he found the unlucky letter. Then we must take the letter to the custom-house. Official number one *viséd* it, and sanded it, and turned me over to official number two. This one looked at the trunk, wrote something on the paper, blotted it with a pinch of dust from the floor, and sent us to official number three, who did a long sum on it, in triplicate, opened a little drawer, took out some sand with an iron spoon, and sprinkled it again. Then number four wrote an illegible signature on each of the three sections, sprinkled on some sand from a box, poured most of the sand on to his desk, and sent us to number five, who verified the computation, wrote his name three times, sanded, and despatched us to number one. The circumlocution was complete. Number one wrote something more, sanded the newspaper he had been reading, and set us free. Now we would get the trunk and be off. By no means; we must trudge back to the station, wait for the clerk to come back from somewhere, pay him some money, give him the letter, and get *his* permit, duly signed and sanded, and then go to the custom-house and carry away the property. It has taken the reader—who has not skipped—some minutes to read this tale. It took me fifteen minutes to write it; it took me six times fifteen minutes to go through the evolutions which it describes.

Feeling sure that I should never climb another mountain, I had brought from Cortina—as a trophy to hang under my Mosel oar—the alpenstock with which I struggled up Tofana: value, twenty-two cents. For convenience I would send it as freight to Havre. To allow for the slowness of the clerks, we assigned an extra three-quarters of an hour for the business of getting it off our hands, besides a half-hour for buying tickets and registering the baggage. In front of the station stands a little guard-house, with the deluding legend, "Expedizione."

"Might I send this stick to Havre?"

"Sicuro!"

"How much will it cost?"

We must ask. The expeditor goes with us to the freight clerk, who answers, "More than it is worth."

"Probably, but how much?"

"How much does it weigh?"

"I don't know."

"Weigh it."

The expeditor hung it to the hook of a steelyard which another man held up: "One kilo" (two pounds). Then, after a calculation: "Two francs."

"Very well; I will stand two francs. No matter about the receipt. Here is the money. Mark it 'Paid,' and send it as soon as possible."

But they manage these things better in Italy. I must go back and see what "Expedizione" really means. I must give the details very clearly, and the official must make out the papers. I might go and get my tickets and fight my baggage through, and then come back. I came back, at the end of a half-hour and of all my patience, and found him still writing. There were three "freight letters," each as long and intricate as a policy of insurance, and two long "declarations" for the custom-house — giving a description, value, etc., etc.* Then we went to the freight clerk, and he signed something, and I signed something (sanded), and the "Expedizione" man demanded three francs and a half. I referred to the contract for two francs.

"Ah! mais! the 'Expedizione' costs a franc and a half."

At last I was free. Everything was attended to, and we had still seven minutes to get our seats. I separated Jane from a poodle with which, and with whose mistress, of course, she had made friends, gathered up my bags and bundles, and started gayly for the train.

As we turned into the corridor we saw the great doors swing to, and our porter shrugged his shoulders.

"But what does it mean?"

"Troppo tardi!"

"It is only ten minutes past nine, and the train leaves at quarter past."

"The doors are closed five minutes before the train starts."

"Then why in—!" But no, the man did not understand English, and no poor words of mine could do justice to the situation. Jane thought otherwise; but then her words are never poor, and on this occasion she showed an approach to genius. As a piece of sketchy characterization, the estimate she expressed of Italian executive ability was worthy of permanent record; but she is overfastidious in such matters, and prefers that her achievement should be permitted to remain our private possession.

The train gone, we demanded to see the station-master. We were taken to his office, and were most politely received. He is a large man and a handsome man, with that suavity and grace of manner for which his race is noted. He listened to our plaint—our vituperation had expended itself behind that closed door—and he encouraged us to express our frank opinion of the administration of Italian railways. I

---

* All concerning twenty-two cents' worth of wood and iron, which has never reached Havre. One of those freight letters has got into a wrong pigeon-hole.

told him of my trunk, and of the stupid fuss about my stick, of the miseries of his baggage-room, and of much incident which one who is travelling in Italy finds ready to his tongue. In such a presence I could not give my opinion its ruder expression, but he took my meaning, and he accepted it in a sympathizing spirit. Unfortunately he could only execute his orders: he deeply regretted that they were such as to cause much annoyance to passengers; he could tell us of other things in which their system was still more at fault; they had made the grave mistake of copying the methods of France, which were full of imperfections, instead of those of England, which were so admirable.

"We are not English; we are American."

"Ah! You are American? I am glad to meet you. Kindly take seats, and tell me of your systems."

Thus the shrewd man turned our thoughts into the didactic channel, always so soothing, and he gave us, by his attention as a listener, almost a compensation for our annoyance. His interest in us grew warm. We had intended to lunch at Verona, and to go on by the next train to Lake Garda, and take the boat for Riva. We would have made a great mistake; for the king and queen were at Verona, and there would be a "festa," which we surely should not miss. Really—we knew our own plans best, but so it seemed to him—we ought by all means to pass the night at Verona. He actually dismissed us in a happy frame of mind.

In a calmer mood I return to my conviction that all we hear of the much-vaunted "regeneration of united Italy" is a mere enthusiast's delusion. No nation tolerating such a system of railway administration as hers holds the germ of regeneration anywhere in its organization. If she is ever to acquire it, she must seek it in the blood of a race to which the management of our best railroads is possible.

Now listen to the tale of our sorrows. See what it implies to lose a train in Venice, and give us your sympathy.

We rowed back to the Piazza; attended the splendid full mass at San Marco; wandered through the unequalled halls of the Ducal Palace — the gorgeous seat of the government of the great republic; lunched at Florian's Caffè; went to Verona in the afternoon; spent the moonlight evening in its vast Roman amphitheatre, and in the crowded square, where the whole town turned out for its promenade, and where a good band gave an open-air concert; passed the next morning among the tombs of the Scaligers, and in the noted Veronese churches; and went comfortably to Peschiera in time for the afternoon boat. The king and queen had left Verona, and of course the "capo di stazione" knew it; but he had made them serve his appeasing purpose all the same.

CHAPTER XIX.

THE LAKES.

WE sat for two hours on the deck of the little steamer, moored to the wharf, and dined there, watching the while the manœuvre of boats with painted lateen-sails, and the work of red-capped sailors; gossiping with the cook, and playing with his dog, and dreaming over the shimmering blue water, and the hot, hazy, far-away shore, where Catullus lived and wrote, and over the fairy crests of the mountains which lead Tyrol down to bathe its feet in the blue waves of Garda.

Some one at the British Association's meeting at Dublin read a paper on the intellect of animals. He cited no case so remarkable as that of Cucino's dog, which lives on this boat. This, and the steamer which runs to Desenzano—fifteen miles away, at the south-west corner of the lake—start from Riva, at the north end of Garda. The dog was familiar with the crews of both, and with the other craft, but he had never made a trip by her. For a long time he watched her course down the other side of the lake, and saw her drawing farther and farther away, until she was hidden by the projecting point. One day, his mind fully settled to its theory, he proceeded to verify it. He marched deliberately over to Desenzano, took passage by the other steamer, came safely to Riva, and went back to his familiar kitchen with an air of entire satisfaction. He could not be induced to make another trip by that boat. He had "done" it, and had no more worlds to conquer in that direction. He had reasoned out a plan of action, and had found his reasoning correct.

Garda is the largest of the Italian lakes—thirty-six miles long. It was our first one, and it must be the bluest lake in the world. It starts in the fertile plain of Lombardy, and, piercing the grand range by which this is sheltered, it runs quite into the heart of the bare-peaked mountains of Austrian Tyrol. All along its eastern shore Italian villages, monasteries, mountains, chapels, vineyards, and chestnut groves give interest to every mile of the journey. After nightfall close-nestling Riva welcomed us to its pleasant lake-side hotel terraces.

Riva has a history such as belongs to all towns of good military position lying on the border-land between the plains of the south and

RIVA, FROM THE PONALE ROAD.

the mountain fastnesses of the north. But it has a beauty — an indescribable lake-side and mountain-foot charm — which attracted us more. Leaving its past to those who are fresher and more eager

students, we contented ourselves with a simple, inactive absorption of
the unsurpassed natural beauty which clusters about this northern nook

TREMOSINE, BY LAKE GARDA.

of the high-walled blue Lago di Garda. We were rowed to its plash-
ing fall of Ponale, and at nightfall we wandered out over its cliff-side
road—a road which absolutely clings to the side of the steep and sometimes overhanging limestone precipices, and is threaded through tunnels like a string through its beads. In more than one place a stone
dropped from its parapet falls yards out into the water, while the rock
above overhangs our heads—Mr. Ruskin to the contrary notwithstand-

ing. Beginning at the level of the lake, it rises by an easy but constant inclination to the very top of the grand rock which sweeps round into the Val di Ledro. As it recedes, it seems scarcely more than a chalk mark along the face of the cliff.

Not the least memorable incident about Riva is the pleasure in leaving it— by no means the pleasure of leaving it, for a more delightful halting-place one need not seek.

Our return was by the Desenzano boat, touching along the bold western bank of the lake, which is more precipitous and far grander than the opposite shore, as it is more prosperous and more populous. Some of its villages are at the top of a precipice apparently a thousand feet above the level of the lake. One of these, Tremosine, a village of some importance, has no other means of communication with the outer world than by a zig-

LEMON GARDEN, LAKE GARDA.

zag foot-path which leads up the almost vertical rock from the steamboat landing.

The great industry, wherever a little soil has been formed at the foot of the mountains, is the cultivation of the lemon, the gardens belonging to the rich nobles of the ducal cities. While the summer climate is well suited to the ripening of the fruit, winter shelter is imperative. The gardens are studded with tall columns of brick masonry, which support the framework of the roof. This is in winter covered with boards, and the vertical openings between the columns are closed with glass. At some points, as in the neighborhood of the town of Limone, these gardens are so extensive as to give a most peculiar effect to the appearance of the shore.

Nothing could be more thoroughly Italian than the graceful, vine-grown, lazy, larger towns at which we touched. At Maderno, where much of the shore front was occupied by shaded terraces set round with pots of aloes and cacti, and where the terraces were occupied by slatternly, dull-looking women, there was a general air of abandonment and uselessness, after the best Italian manner. Happy this people who while away their dreamy and untidy summers under the soft breezes that sweep this widest stretch of Italian water!

Desenzano, where we landed, has not responded even to the summons of the steam-whistle. Judging from the manner of those who would have relieved me of the burden of my field-glass during the pleasant stroll to the station, I should say that beggary was its chief remaining industry. Of the station it is not worth while to say more than that it belongs to the railway which leads from Venice, and that it possessed no time-table by which we could determine our route and our connections. Under this same method of administration, instead of spending two hours at Brescia, as we might have done, and where we might have breakfasted like Christians, we were stranded for a longer time in an unfinished station-house in Southern Illinois. They called it Rovato, the people spoke Italian, the beggars were polite, and three car-loads of Italian soldiers who belonged to our party were playing morra—uno! ott! chink! bang! thump! and there go your ten soldi. But for all that, I have never seen its match for newness and crudity save in our own benighted Egypt.

All things come to an end; so did our stifling and hungry halt, and we trundled on through the rich foot-hill country, among vineyards and campanili, past Palazznolo and Bergamo, then beside the premonitory and enticing waters which lead down to Lecco, thence

LIMONE, LAKE GARDA.

in an omnibus through unheeded streets, and hurriedly to our journey's end—the deck of a Como steamer. Here at last the spirit of haste was laid. Fast or slow, early or late, it mattered nothing now. We were afloat on the Lake of Como.

The afternoon was only so far gone as to give us lengthened shadows; the sky was clear, the air was soft, and we had gone out of this world into that realm of fancy where prose and poetry, art and photography, had builded our visions—

> "A clear lake, margined by fruits of gold
> And whispering myrtles, glassing softest skies
> As cloudless, save with rare and roseate shadows,
> As I would have thy fate."

Evening fell slowly; each headland, each hamlet, and each mountain-top became more and more unreal in the fading light, and as the low stars began to glimmer out of the fleeting western gold, we climbed the broad white steps of

> "A palace lifting to eternal heaven
> Its marble walls, from out a glossy bower
> Of coolest foliage, musical with birds. . . .
> The perfumed light
> Stole through the mists of alabaster lamps,
> And every air was heavy with the sighs
> Of orange groves, and music from sweet lutes,
> And murmurs of low fountains that gush forth
> I' the midst of roses."

For even this too was added to our cup. Our first halt was at the regal Villa Frizzoni, rich with every luxury that architecture and Italian lake-side gardening could, at the behest of wealth, offer for the acceptance of a wife. By that grace of good fortune by which the traveller often profits, the Villa Frizzoni, unspoiled of all its luxury, has become the "Grand Hotel Bellaggio," and all the season through its halls and balconies and terraces, and its orange-shaded walks, are gay with the life and dress and music of a pleasure-seeking throng. If the imagination, revelling in the charm of Como, needs the further stimulus of princes, baronen, contessi, and Ticino nurse-maids, they are all here, to be had for the looking.

Regarded with the cold eye of the captious traveller, this hotel fills every requirement, and from the American stand-point its scale of charges is incredibly low. The best that Saratoga can offer is mean and commonplace compared with this, yet a bachelor must spend more there for his top-story cell and his caravansary feeding than need here a reasonable couple, content with a charming second story front room,

SAN GIOVANNI, BELLAGGIO, ON LAKE COMO.

and with simple claret at the delicate and exquisitely served table-d'hôte.

We were easily tempted to borrow from the few days assigned to Paris, and to tarry here until conscience drove us forth. I had reserved for my last afternoon's walk a visit to the Villa Serbelloni, perched high up on the promontory between the Lecco and the Como arms of the lake. It was a question of taking this walk in a sad rain or not taking it at all, for in the morning we must surely leave. Leave! As easily leave Eden itself. Conscience and duty all forgotten, I incontinently engaged quarters for three days more in this rambling, old nobleman's house, now transformed into a quiet, homely hotel.

We had rowed over the lake to the meretricious Villa Carlotta, we had lounged at Cadenabbia, and we had drunk in all the riparian delights of this delicious inland sea, but we had conceived no such wealth of beauty, of situation, of vegetation, and of scrupulous horticulture as greeted us here at every turn. It is useless to attempt description; I simply commend this charmed spot as the best earthly representation of a veritable fairy-land. The garden of Serbelloni

LECCO.

is formal and artificial to the last degree; but its formality is ennobled by the majestic rock on whose summit it rests; and its art has made cunning use of the vegetation of every zone. Our fellow-guests, though few, were no less interesting than those we had left at the water-side.

It carried us back many a long year, and brought up the memories of a mad enthusiasm, to see again, somewhat saddened by age and care, but still the same, that face which we all knew so well when her wonderful voice and her magnetic presence stirred the most hidden chords of the thousands of hearts which beat in unison under the great dome of Castle Garden in 1851. She is a grandmother now, but we who had heard that matchless song saw her only as the Jenny Lind of our youth.

It is something in favor of these hotels that they lie at the edge of the quaint old town of Bellaggio. These Continental towns seem to be exempt from the influence which, with us, assimilates all communities to their conspicuous surroundings. Here, whither rich and extravagant tourists have flocked for years, their wealth and extravagance have had absolutely no effect upon the simple people whom they daily elbow in its narrow arcaded streets. Even the arts by which the tourist's money is enticed into their careful pouches are practised with a simplicity and an unspoiled and unassuming politeness which make the payment of their modest demands a pleasure. I have in mind now a sturdy and hearty oarsman, rich with more or less authentic gossip of those whom he has seen and of those whom he has served, and as proud of his position of a Bellaggio peasant—a leader among the *bassi genti*—as he would be of ducal honors if he wore them. He has sat face to face, and has chatted familiarly, with thousands of men and women of every rank that travels; yet he carries himself with the dignity of conscious worth, and with the grace and nátive elegance of an Italian country man.

We crossed the hills to Lugano in the coupé of a diligence, in a light rain, which, as our occasional glimpses of the Simplon and the Bernardino showed, was the first autumn snow on the higher mountains. Still in the rain, we sailed down the beautiful mountain lake to the town of Lugano. This journey was made interesting and memorable by one of those sudden and charming companionships which spring up in the fertile soil of a traveller's experiences. We parted at the pier, and we may never meet again, but our memory of this lovely Italian-Swiss lake will always recall our genial and most congenial Briton.

It would be aside from my purpose to detail our experiences at Lugano and on Lago Maggiore. They continued and they varied the impressions received on Garda, and made eternal on Como. It is almost futile to write fresh lines at this late day of what has delighted the scribes of all times. Even in the first century of our era, the

A STREET IN BELLAGGIO.

younger Pliny wrote to his friend Caninius Rufus: "What are you doing at Como? Do you study, hunt, or fish, or all three together? For on our beloved lake one can do all these. Her waters afford fish, her wooded heights game, and her deep solitude quiet for study. But whatever you do, I envy you, and I cannot restrain the confession that it makes my heart heavy not to be able to share that with you for which I pine as a sick man for a cooling drink, a bath, or a living spring. Shall I tear with violence these closely fitting bonds, if no

FROM THE VILLA SERBELLONI.

other solution is possible? Ah! I fear never. For before old occupations are ended, new ones are thrust upon me, and thus link after link is added to the chain of endless toil which holds me here enthralled. Farewell." From Pliny's time to ours the literature of all lands has lingered over these beautiful lakes.

Our route led us to Milan, where we were favored with that rare clear atmosphere which reveals to the Lombard plain one of the most majestic of the world's sights. The Venetian Alps, the peaks of the Carinthian range, the great Dolomites, the Gross Glockner, the Oertler, the entire range of Swiss peaks to Mont Blanc, with seven-peaked Monte Rosa in the foreground, the Cottian Alps, with their pyramidal Monte Viso, the Maritime Alps, the Apennines, and the Euganean Hills, near Padua, closed almost the entire horizon with the grandest mountain chain of Europe. This view in its entirety is rarely seen. Our good fortune was not evanescent, for no cloud, no slightest film of vapor, came to screen this glorious panorama from all our long road to Turin. Throughout the whole day the grand army of mountain-tops marshalled itself for review, the majestic peaks marching slowly to their ever-changing positions as we sped swiftly on our way. The rich irrigated sub-Alpine plain was their parade-ground, and against the broad blue banner of an Italian sky stood the sharp outlines of their icy helmets. As the daylight died away, the red glory of the Alpine glow still lifted them out of the coming night.

CHAPTER XX.

THE VAUDOIS VALLEYS.—THE WALDENSES.

Turin was for us only a halting-place, and not even the splendor of its famed Superga could delay us. We hastened on to those grim valleys where, resisting the wicked might of man, the children of God through so many sad centuries withstood the fiercest persecutions of Rome, and handed down unspoiled, from generation to generation, the stern hard faith of the pure Apostolic Church. As the assumptions and encroachments of Rome turned the power of the Church to the worldly aggrandizement of its rulers, those who held to the primitive faith were forced to seek shelter in obscurity. The rugged mountain valleys on the borders of Piedmont and Dauphiny became their ultimate retreat. Here, long before the protest of Luther, they held the torch of the ancient religion which he labored to restore. Here was the birthplace of Romish persecution, and here were concentrated, from 1308 to the downfall of the Inquisition, all the horrors of which fiendish fanaticism has been capable. Once, and once only, was the last remnant of this chosen people driven from these valleys to the refuge of Calvinistic Switzerland; but their *Glorieuse Rentrée* under Arnaud re-established the old faith in its ancient seat, whence, to this day, it sends its evangelists to every corner of Italy.

It is of the persecutions of this people that Milton wrote his grandest sonnet:

> "Avenge, O Lord! Thy slaughter'd saints whose bones
> Lie scatter'd on the Alpine mountains cold:
> E'en them, who kept Thy truth so pure of old,
> When all our fathers worshipp'd stocks and stones, .
> Forget not; in Thy book record their groans,
> Who were Thy sheep, and in their ancient fold
> Slain by the bloody Piedmontese, that roll'd

> Mother with infant down the rocks. Their moans
> The vales redoubled to the hills, and they
> To heaven. Their martyr'd blood and ashes sow
> O'er all the Italian fields, where still doth sway
> The triple tyrant, that from these may grow
> An hundred-fold, who, having learned Thy way,
> Early may fly the Babylonian woe."

The history of the Piedmontese Protestants is well told in "The Israel of the Alps," by Dr. Muston. It may be briefly sketched here. These people — the Waldenses, or the Vaudois — occupy what are known as the Vaudois Valleys, in the Cottian Alps, about thirty miles south-west of Turin, between Mont Cenis and Monte Viso. The central valleys are Pellice, Luzerna, and Angrogna. The Vaudois (the Valdesi — dwellers in the valleys) are known by existing sermons of their pastors, dated 1120; and Peter Waldo, the reformer, of Lyons, doubtless took his name from them, not, as has been assumed, giving his name to them: he was Peter the Vaudois. The Vaudois are not to be confounded with the inhabitants of the Canton de Vaud of Switzerland. Their earliest record is of the year 1100, but they believe their ancestors through every age, from the apostolic time to the present, to have been protesters against the corruptions of the Church, and the depositaries of the simple Gospel faith.

About the middle of the twelfth century there appeared two important Vaudois documents: a translation of the New Testament and "La Nobla Leyczon." These are in the Romance language, which is the *patois* still spoken in the valleys. The "Noble Lesson," a poem of five hundred lines, is a summary of Scripture history and doctrines, and teaches toleration and religious freedom.

In 1517, the year of Luther's denunciation, the Archbishop of Turin drew up an enumeration of the immemorial belief and protest of the Vaudois Church. These are its points:

The Vaudois received the Scriptures as their only rule of faith. They rejected the doctrines introduced by the popes and priests. They declared that tithes and first-fruits are not due to the clergy. They disapproved of the consecration of churches. They denied that men needed the intercession of saints. They rejected purgatory and masses for the dead. They denied that priests have the power to forgive sins.

They opposed the confessional. They protested against the worship of the Virgin and saints. They rejected the use of holy-water; condemned indulgences; and ascribed the doctrine of purgatory to the covetousness of priests. They abhorred the use of the sign of the cross and the worship of images. They denied that wicked men could be representatives of Christ. They disowned the authority of the Church of Rome, and they believed that prayer in private houses is as acceptable as prayer in churches.

The declaration of these principles brought upon them the anathemas of Rome, and papal bulls were issued commanding Catholic princes to wage war against them. In 1485 a bull of Innocent VIII., enjoining the extermination of the Vandois, absolved those who should take up the cross against them "from all ecclesiastical pains and penalties, general and particular . . . releasing them from any oath they might have taken, legitimatizing their title to any property they might have illegally acquired, and promising remission of all their sins to such as should kill any heretic." It outlawed the Vandois, annulled their contracts, and empowered all persons to take possession of their property. In the persecutions which followed, and which recurred at intervals for centuries, human infamy reached its climax. I quote parts of a single paragraph from Muston:

"There is no town in Piedmont under a Vandois pastor where some of our brethren have not been put to death. Jordan Terbano was burned alive at Susa; Hippolite Rossiero at Turin; Michael Goneto, an octogenarian, at Sarcena; Villermin Ambrosio hanged on the Col di Meano; Hugo Chiambs, of Fenestrelle, had his entrails torn from his living body at Turin; Peter Geymarali, of Bobbio, in like manner had his entrails taken out in Luzerna, and a fierce cat thrust in their place to torture him further; Maria Romano was buried alive at Rocca-patia; Magdalena Fanno underwent the same fate at San Giovanni; Susanna Michelini was bound hand and foot, and left to perish of cold and hunger on the snow at Sarcena; Bartolomeo Fache, gashed with sabres, had the wounds filled up with quick-lime, and perished thus in agony at Fenile; Daniel Michelini had his tongue torn out at Bobbo for having praised God; James Baridari perished covered with sulphureous matches, which had been forced into his flesh under the nails, between the fingers, in the nostrils, in the lips, and over all his body, and then lighted; Daniel Revelli had his mouth filled with gunpowder, which being lighted blew his head to pieces; ... Sara Rostignol was slit open from the legs to the bosom, and left so to perish on the road between Eyral and Luzerna; Anna Charbonnier was impaled, and carried thus on a pike from San Giovanni to La Torre."

In 1630-'31 the plague invaded the valleys, and swept away more than 12,000 persons—about one-half of the whole population. In La Torre more than fifty families became completely extinct. Of the seventeen pastors, only two venerable and infirm old men escaped death. It then became necessary to import French-speaking ministers from Dauphiny and from Geneva. The government thereupon, as a further means of repression, prohibited the performance of the Vaudois service in any language but French, and this tongue was learned by the whole people, and is retained by them to this day.

More than once was the population reduced by war and oppression from its normal standard of about 25,000 to 4000 or 5000. Yet they always remained steadfast in their faith, and held to their ancient traditions, rising stronger after each invasion, and always regaining their ruined prosperity.

Some of the episodes of their wars are marvellous to read. Their most noted hero Gianavello, with a band of less than twenty followers, sometimes with only half a dozen, defeated whole armies of invaders; and the Flying Company at Pra del Tor overthrew the Count de la Trinità, who marched against them with three columns, numbering more than seven thousand men. The almost uniform success of these little bands of rude mountaineers operating against large armies of disciplined troops has naturally produced among the Vaudois the belief that it was not their prowess in action which prevailed, but the design of God to preserve the germ of true religion in their keeping.

They gained frequent respite for the recovery of their prosperity and the restoring of their population by the contests in which the Dukes of Savoy were so often engaged with other princes. It was at the revocation of the Edict of Nantes, to which the Duke of Savoy, Victor Amadeo II., was reluctantly forced to accede, that the remnant of the population was compelled to accept exile into Switzerland. Of 14,000 persons 3000 only survived. They were liberally helped by the Protestants of England and Holland. Recovering their health, they were afflicted with the homesickness so peculiar to mountaineers, but were detained by force, and were widely dispersed through the Protestant states of Germany.

William of Orange, the head of the Protestant League against France, was visited at the Hague by Henri Arnaud, the pastor and leader of the Vaudois. He counselled that they should return and attempt to regain their valleys by force, supplying them at the same time with considerable funds. The refugees assembled, between eight and nine hundred in number, leaving their wives and children to the care of the Swiss, crossing Lake Leman in the night of August 16th, 1689. Led by their pastor-captain, they crossed the Alps, and descended into Italy near Susa.

After sixteen days' march, having beaten several strong detachments of the enemy, they established themselves at Bobi, where they remained unmolested during the winter, but by May they were reduced to four hundred men. They were again assailed, but they resisted and struggled against every force invading the valley, until the Duke of Savoy, abandoning his alliance with France, and joining the Protestant League, restored them to their homes and liberties, recalled their wives and children, and ended the last of thirty-two wars for liberty and conscience. One hundred and sixty years later, Carlo Alberto, giving a constitution to his people, insured the continuance of religious liberty.

It was with no ordinary traveller's interest that we went to visit the scenes of all those centuries of heroic life and more heroic death, and the renowned centre from which Protestantism in Italy is pushing its steady advance. We drove from the railway station at Pinerolo, an hour's journey, to Torre Pellice, which is the seat of the Vaudois College and the chief town of the valleys.

Though in Italy still, we found among the Protestants the universal use of the French language, and among the educated classes a familiarity with English, due to the Scotch education of the pastors. It is no mild modern Protestantism which prevails here, softened by the spirit of indulgence we know so well at home, but a stern Scotch Puritanism — rigid, intolerant, uncompromising, and grim — ground into the sturdy souls of the people by long generations of martyrdom and oppression. It is a faith so real and so commanding that it rings like a clarion in the zeal of the trained evangelists, who, scattered throughout the kingdom, echo the eternal reverberations of the blood-stained mountain-sides where their fathers died for the cause they advocate.

It seems to me that the first impression of any considerate person coming to the Vaudois valleys with a fresh recollection of what we are taught to consider the necessary conditions of civilized life must be one of humiliation. We may find similarly hard conditions of living in many of our remote districts, but we find them accompanied by a dulness and stolidity which make it seem a matter of indifference whether they are ameliorated or not; or we find them resisted or struggled against with that determination to seek improvement which makes our people so ambitious and so restless.

Here in these hard, bleak valleys a frugality of which we can hardly have conception is practised with a calmness and serenity that betoken an aim of life far other than physical improvement. In the town of Torre this is less conspicuous than elsewhere; but even here cultivated, enthusiastic, happy men and women, eager in the great pursuit of their lives, practise the genial graces of refined society, and exert a wide-spread influence, which is powerful even against that of Rome, amidst an almost entire absence of the advantages which come of wealth, and which are so often regarded as indispensable.

Catechised as to their belief, these people develop the most rigid formulas of orthodoxy, that which we have known among the coldest, hardest, most unsympathizing New Englanders. But the blood of the South runs warm in their veins, and their religion, severe though it is, can only check—it cannot cover nor repress—the geniality of their Italian natures. It is the rigidity of the North made mellow with Latin warmth, and sweetened with the grace and amiability of Italy. I know no people of great wealth who seem to get so much out of their lives that is worth the getting as do these simple, pious, God-fearing Vaudois.

CHAPTER XXI.

INTO THE HIGHER VALLEYS.

DESIRING to visit the valley of Angrogna, the great retreat during the invasions of the land, and the scene of the most terrible battles, I was commended to the pastor of the village, who has the care of the scattered population of the large parish. It was a long, hard walk up the valley, and a hot one. A very plain little Protestant "temple" and a few poor houses constitute the village of Angrogna, which is dominated by a larger Catholic church, whose priest does his worst to counteract the cherished heresy here in its ancient stronghold.

A child directed me to the pastor's door—a great solid wooden door in a fortress-like stone wall. Entering, I was greeted pleasantly by the cheerful mother of the house, who ushered me into a scantily furnished parlor, clean, bright, and pleasant. Presently the pastor appeared, received me with the greatest cordiality, and lent himself at once to my desire for guidance and information.

I have rarely been more impressed in any interview. He told me with the greatest frankness of the difficulties with which he has to contend in eking out a support for his large family in a parish where all are poor, and where many can give nothing to the support of the Church beyond cordial good wishes and the scantiest contributions of food. A little money is given him by the General Synod, but it is very little, and this man's incessant pastoral duties make it impossible for him to ameliorate his condition by any form of profitable work. It is to gratify no curiosity that I repeat what he told me of his circumstances, but rather to illustrate, by a striking and extreme example, what I have said of life in these valleys generally.

I was regaled in the most hospitable manner with the best that the house afforded—a thin, simple wine, bread, a hard sort of cheese, and boiled chestnuts, of which I was urged to take my fill, as I would find no other opportunity to eat during the day's journey. What was given me is the best of their diet, and, except for potatoes and salad, it covers the limit of its variety for all the secular days of the week. On Sundays they usually, but not always, have meat. There was no suggestion that the diet was not sufficient and satisfactory, and the family seemed to be in robust and hearty health. The physical labor of the pastor himself must be very severe. His parish reaches for miles back on the mountains, and far up into steep and rugged valleys. He has three separate churches and schools under his charge, and his sick and poor are scattered far and wide on every hand.

Foot-paths and bridle-paths offer the only means of communication, and he is liable, day and night, winter and summer, in good weather and in bad, to be summoned forth for a long, hard tramp to the house of a sick or dying parishioner. All this he described as merely incidental to a life of necessary and useful service, in which he is content and happy. A friend had recently presented him with a young donkey, which is already able to give him a short lift on his journeys; and which, as it matures, and as he grows old, will carry him to Pra del Tor and back. He was happy over this acquisition, but anxious as to his ability to nourish the beast.

Regarded in a certain light, there is nothing remarkable about this tale of a robust man's life and circumstances; but viewed with reference to the stock to which he belongs, and to the history of the wonderful struggle of his race, it seems to me not far removed from heroism. The world is full of well-paid positions, seeking for the education, intelligence, executive ability, and fortitude which mark the character of this cheerful and zealous pastor of Angrogna; but the old call of the Spirit rings in his ears, and stirs his blood as it stirred that of the martyrs of old, and he stays and finds his happiness and his delight in answering its behests.

I talked with him about the condition of the people, and about the ceaseless efforts of the Catholic Church to destroy the Protestant supremacy in the valleys. Poverty, or rather the simplicity of living, is extreme. The climate is much more severe than at Torre; the soil in the main is poor and thin; the cattle are stunted; and the facilities for irrigation and the habit of its use seem to constitute the chief agricultural advantage of the country. The chestnut grows well, and is a main reliance as food. Without it there would often be much suffering.

The Roman Catholic Church has by no means given up its effort at supremacy. The best sites are secured for its churches and convents; its abundant and skilfully-managed alms-giving is a powerful resource in so poor a country; and its control over the industrial populations, which quarrying and manufactures have brought to the neighborhood, is shrewdly used for the corruption of the young men and women of the Protestant communities. At Pra del Tor—the Holy Land of the Vaudois—the priests have established a foundling hospital, which threatens the stability of the rising generation of native children by the insidious influence of contact and companionship. This more hidden and surreptitious persecution is met as resolutely and firmly and cunningly as were the physical assaults of old; and thus far its influence has not been great.

As it was Saturday, the pastor could not go with me, as I had hoped; but he recited the heroic deeds of which Pra del Tor had been the theatre, and invested it with a historic sublimity which mere reading could not give. He lent me the keys of the temples I should see, and directed me on my way.

It was a two hours' walk, mainly upward, over a rough bridle-path, with here and there a house, and here and there a little mill driven by the abundant waters of the tumbling stream. Toward the end of the journey the path passes between steep rocky banks, climbs the edge of a precipitous hill-side, and opens into the valley of Pra del Tor—that valley which more than once held all that was left of the Piedmontese Vaudois, who, driven from their farms and their villages, gathered here for mutual support and defence. Even here, while awaiting the destruction which seemed impending, they established their schools, and kept up the education of their evangelists.

On a high rock, overlooking the cluster of houses, stands a well-built modern temple, the gift of a friend in England to commemorate the defenders of the valley against Trinità's overwhelming force. All else is meagre, bare, and stern. It is hard to see how even this small population can subsist in such a land, and it is almost incredible that a people who generation after generation have been subjected to such trying conditions of life should resist, as they steadily do, the seductions of an organization able and ready to improve their condition, or to remove them to a more fertile district. It is these considerations which everywhere impress the visitor with the sturdiness of character which an old faith, cemented by long ages of martyrdom, has been able to produce.

My climb made it seem quite necessary that I should have food before returning. All that I could get was milk. This was served to me on the stone stair leading to a house door, and in a rude earthenware pan. As I drank it, with a coarse iron spoon, a starved kitten came with a longing mew, and lapped greedily the little puddle which I poured into a hollow of the stone. I never saw such a hungry cat, and evidently the family never saw such a hungry man, for they commented freely on the eagerness of my feeding. Poor though they were, and unaccustomed as they seemed to be to such a lavish use of milk, they would accept no compensation for their hospitality, and I could only make a trifling present to their child.

Here, and on my return, the people whom I met were most cordial and friendly, and they answered every question as to the difficulty of making a living on such a soil with an evident unconsciousness that it implies the least hardship. Those who were returning from their fields generally bore heavy burdens of firewood or grain; and one donkey that I met taking grist to mill carried at least 800 pounds of grain, picking his way cautiously over the rocky path. Parts of the valley were heavily wooded and of great beauty, but everything about the scattered villages and farms seemed dismal and forbidding.

On Sunday we drove eight miles up the Pellice Valley to attend church at Bobi, where, in 1689, after the *Glorieuse Rentrée*, Arnand and his followers took the oath of fidelity, and celebrated divine service in their own temple for the first time since their banishment.

"The enthusiasm of the moment was irrepressible; they chanted the 74th Psalm to the clash of arms, and Henri Arnand, mounting the pulpit, with a sword in one hand and a Bible in the other, preached from the 129th Psalm, and once more declared in the face of heaven that he would never resume his pastoral office in patience and peace until he should witness the restoration of his brethren to their ancient and rightful settlements."

The temple was a bare room, with unpainted pulpit and benches, where the women sat in one place and the men in another. The women wore a costume of which a white cap with wide double fluted ruffles was a conspicuous part, the young girls—those who had not been confirmed—wearing black caps instead. The men were men whom I had known in my childhood in the orthodox churches of Western Connecticut, smooth-shaven—for Sunday—wrinkled, uncompromising countrymen. The older men generally wore blue jean dress-coats with metal buttons and high collars. When the psalms were given out, they took loud-clasping iron cases from their pockets, and put on their steel-bowed spectacles. Puritanism is stronger than race, or climate, or time. It was like sitting again among the hard-handed farmers who used to throng the old Congregational church in New Canaan.

The illusion was hardly dispelled—so strong was the resemblance in face and dress and manner—when the young precentor mounted to the reading-desk and read a chapter of the New Testament in French. It was strengthened when he gave out the psalm, pitched the key, and started the congregation in the droning monotone of its chanted praise. The sermon was preached in the purest French by a most Italian-looking pastor from Messina. It was an earnest appeal to humility, and a warning not to permit their pride in their ancestry and in the venerable antiquity of their faith, to blind them to the obligations to which the essence of that faith compelled them. After the service there followed the silent and hardly sociable loitering about the door which characterizes the congregations of our own country churches, but far less curiosity was evinced and more politeness was shown toward the differently attired strangers who had come to join in their service.

During our stay in the valleys we were shown the admirable orphanage at Torre, where Mr. Sankey's hymns were sung in French and Italian, and where the most careful training is given in the little arts and industries of common life. We saw, too, the Vaudois College, where are trained the pastors who are to have charge of the flocks scattered throughout Italy, and the evangelists who are to plant in the dark corners of the land the most promising germ of Italian regeneration. It is a simple school, ill furnished with the modern appliances of education, but rich in the zeal and enthusiasm with which its leaders keep steadily in view the great aim of its foundation.

The college, and the cause of Protestantism generally, owe most efficient aid to the liberality and earnestness of Major Beckwith, an English officer, who devoted his fortune and many of the last years of his life to their advancement. Much has been done by the liberality of other British friends, and there can surely be no channel to-day into which those who have the interest of reformed religion at heart can so effectively turn their contributions. The Vaudois schools are established in all parts of Italy, even in Calabria and Sicily and in Rome itself, and they offer the chief existing hope of the education of the people in what is necessary to an improved civilization.

Victor Emanuel—*il Re Galantuomo*—in spite of his Catholicism, was a steadfast and persistent friend of the Vaudois, believing that they offered the best promise for the improvement of his people. Humbert has given fresh assurances that his father's policy in this regard shall be maintained, not in the interest of religion, but in the interest of liberty and of enlightenment.

THE END.

ILLUSTRATED BOOKS OF TRAVEL

PUBLISHED BY

HARPER & BROTHERS.

☞ *For a full list of Books of Travel published by* HARPER & BROTHERS, *see* HARPERS' CATALOGUE, *which may be had gratuitously on application to the Publishers personally, or by letter enclosing Nine Cents.*

☞ HARPER & BROTHERS *will send any of the following works by mail, postage prepaid, to any part of the United States, on receipt of the price.*

Waring's Tyrol.
Tyrol, and the Skirt of the Alps. By GEORGE E. WARING, Jr. Illustrated. 8vo, Cloth. (*Just Ready.*)

Cesnola's Cyprus.
Cyprus: its Ancient Cities, Tombs, and Temples. A Narrative of Researches and Excavations during Ten Years' Residence in that Island. By General LOUIS PALMA DI CESNOLA, Member of the Royal Academy of Sciences, Turin; Hon. Member of the Royal Society of Literature, London, &c. With Portrait, Maps, and 400 Illustrations. 8vo, Cloth, Extra, Gilt Tops and Uncut Edges, $7 50.

Stanley's Through the Dark Continent.
Through the Dark Continent; or, The Sources of the Nile, Around the Great Lakes of Equatorial Africa, and Down the Livingstone River to the Atlantic Ocean. With 149 Illustrations and 10 Maps. By HENRY M. STANLEY. 2 vols., 8vo, Cloth, $10 00; Sheep, $12 00; Half Morocco, $15 00. (*Sold by Subscription only.*)

Bartlett's From Egypt to Palestine.
From Egypt to Palestine: through Sinai, the Wilderness, and the South Country. Observations of a Journey made with Special Reference to the History of the Israelites. By the Rev. S. C. BARTLETT, D.D., LL.D., President of Dartmouth College. With Maps and Illustrations. 8vo, Cloth, $3 50.

Lady Blunt's Bedouin Tribes of the Euphrates.
Bedouin Tribes of the Euphrates. By Lady ANNE BLUNT. Edited, with a Preface, and some Account of the Arabs and their Horses, by W. S. B. Map and Sketches by the Author. 8vo, Cloth, $2 50.

Benjamin's Atlantic Islands.
The Atlantic Islands as Resorts for Health and Pleasure. By S. G. W. BENJAMIN. Illustrated. 8vo, Cloth, $3 00.

Du Chaillu's Land of the Midnight Sun.
The Land of the Midnight Sun. Travels in Sweden, Norway, and Lapland, 1871-77. By PAUL B. DU CHAILLU. 2 vols., 8vo. (*In Press.*)

Thomson's Voyage of the "Challenger."

The Voyage of the "Challenger." *The Atlantic:* An Account of the General Results of the Voyage during the Year 1873 and the Early Part of the Year 1876. By Sir C. WYVILLE THOMSON, F.R.S. With a Portrait of the Author engraved by C. H. Jeens, many Colored Maps, Temperature Charts, and Illustrations engraved by J. D. Cooper, from Drawings by J. J. Wyld. Published by Authority of the Lords Commissioners of the Admiralty. 2 vols., 8vo, Cloth, $12 00.

Spry's Cruise of the "Challenger."

The Cruise of Her Majesty's Ship "Challenger." Voyages over many Seas, Scenes in many Lands. By W. J. J. SPRY, R.N. With Map and Illustrations. Crown 8vo, Cloth, $2 00.

Vincent's Land of the White Elephant.

The Land of the White Elephant: Sights and Scenes in Southeastern Asia. A Personal Narrative of Travel and Adventure in Farther India, embracing the Countries of Burma, Siam, Cambodia, and Cochin-China (1871-2). By FRANK VINCENT, Jr. Magnificently Illustrated with Maps, Plans, and numerous Woodcuts. 8vo, Cloth, $3 50.

Wallace's Malay Archipelago.

The Malay Archipelago: the Land of the Orang-Utan and the Bird of Paradise. A Narrative of Travel, 1854-62. With Studies of Man and Nature. By ALFRED RUSSEL WALLACE. With Maps and numerous Illustrations. Crown 8vo, Cloth, $2 50.

Baker's Ismailïa.

Ismailïa: a Narrative of the Expedition to Central Africa for the Suppression of the Slave-Trade, organized by ISMAIL, KHEDIVE OF EGYPT. By Sir SAMUEL WHITE BAKER, PASHA, M.A., F.R.S., F.R.G.S., Major-General of the Ottoman Empire, late Governor-General of the Equatorial Nile Basin, &c., &c. With Maps, Portraits, and upward of 50 full-page Illustrations by Zwecker and Durand. 8vo, Cloth, $5 00; Half Calf, $7 25.

Cameron's Across Africa.

Across Africa. By VERNEY LOVETT CAMERON, C.B., D.C.L., Commander Royal Navy, Gold Medalist Royal Geographical Society, &c. With a Map and numerous Illustrations. 8vo, Cloth, $5 00.

Orton's Andes and the Amazon.

The Andes and the Amazon; or, Across the Continent of South America. By JAMES ORTON, Ph.D., late Professor of Natural History in Vassar College, Poughkeepsie, N. Y.; Corresponding Member of the Academy of Natural Sciences, Philadelphia, and of the Lyceum of Natural History, N. Y. Third Edition, Revised and Enlarged, containing Notes of a Second Journey Across the Continent from Pará to Lima and Lake Titicaca. With Two Maps and numerous Illustrations. 8vo, Cloth, $3 00.

Palmer's Desert of the Exodus.

The Desert of the Exodus. Journeys on Foot in the Wilderness of the Forty Years' Wanderings; undertaken in Connection with the Ordnance Survey of Sinai and the Palestine Exploration Fund. By E. H. PALMER, M.A., Lord Almoner's Professor of Arabic, and Fellow of St. John's College, Cambridge. With Maps and numerous Illustrations, from Photographs and Drawings taken on the Spot by the Sinai Survey Expedition and C. F. Tyrwhitt Drake. Crown 8vo, Cloth, $3 00.

Hazard's Santo Domingo.

Santo Domingo, Past and Present; with a Glance at Hayti. By SAMUEL HAZARD. Maps and Illustrations. Crown 8vo, Cloth, $3 50.

Pike's Sub-Tropical Rambles.

Sub-Tropical Rambles in the Land of the Aphanapteryx: Personal Experiences, Adventures, and Wanderings in and about the Island of Mauritius. By NICHOLAS PIKE. Handsomely Illustrated. 8vo, Cloth, $3 50.

Squier's Peru.

Peru: Incidents of Travel and Exploration in the Land of the Incas. By E. G. SQUIER, M.A., F.S.A., late U. S. Commissioner to Peru. Illustrated. 8vo, Cloth, $5 00.

Griffis's The Mikado's Empire.

The Mikado's Empire. Book I. History of Japan, from 660 B.C. to 1872 A.D. Book II. Personal Experiences, Observations, and Studies in Japan, 1870-1874. By WILLIAM ELLIOT GRIFFIS, A.M., late of the Imperial University of Tōkiō, Japan. Copiously Illustrated. 8vo, Cloth, $4 00; Half Calf, $6 25.

Thomson's Malacca, Indo-China, and China.

The Straits of Malacca, Indo-China, and China; or, Ten Years' Travels, Adventures, and Residence Abroad. By J. THOMSON, F.R.G.S. With over 60 Illustrations from the Author's own Photographs and Sketches. 8vo, Cloth, $4 00.

MacGahan's Campaigning on the Oxus.

Campaigning on the Oxus and the Fall of Khiva. By J. A. MACGAHAN. With Map and Illustrations. 8vo, Cloth, $3 50.

Tristram's Land of Moab.

The Land of Moab: Travels and Discoveries on the East Side of the Dead Sea and the Jordan. By H. B. TRISTRAM, M.A., LL.D., F.R.S., Honorary Canon of Durham. With a Chapter on the Persian Palace of Mashita, by JAMES FERGUSON, F.R.S. With Map and Illustrations. Crown 8vo, Cloth, $2 50.

Van-Lennep's Bible Lands.

Bible Lands: their Modern Customs and Manners illustrative of Scripture. By the Rev. HENRY J. VAN-LENNEP, D.D. Illustrated with upward of 350 Wood Engravings and two Colored Maps. 838 pp., 8vo, Cloth, $5 00; Sheep, $6 00; Half Calf, $8 00.

Nordhoff's Northern California, Oregon, and the Sandwich Islands.

Northern California, Oregon, and the Sandwich Islands. By CHARLES NORDHOFF. Illustrated. 8vo, Cloth, $2 50.

Nordhoff's California.

California: for Health, Pleasure, and Residence. A Book for Travellers and Settlers. By CHARLES NORDHOFF. Illustrated. 8vo, Cloth, $2 50.

Kingsley's West Indies.

At Last: a Christmas in the West Indies. By CHARLES KINGSLEY. Illustrated. 12mo, Cloth, $1 50.

Bishop Haven's Mexico.

Our Next-Door Neighbor. Recent Sketches of Mexico. By the Rev. GILBERT HAVEN, D.D., Bishop in the M. E. Church. With Maps and Illustrations. 8vo, Cloth, $3 50.

Bush's Reindeer, Dogs, and Snow-shoes.

Reindeer, Dogs, and Snow-shoes: a Journal of Siberian Travel and Explorations made in the Years 1865-'67. By RICHARD J. BUSH, late of the Russo-American Telegraph Expedition. Illustrated. Crown 8vo, Cloth, $3 00.

Prime's Around the World.

Around the World. By EDWARD D. G. PRIME, D.D. With numerous Illustrations. Crown 8vo, Cloth, $3 00.

Schweinfurth's Heart of Africa.

The Heart of Africa; or, Three Years' Travels and Adventures in the Unexplored Regions of the Centre of Africa. From 1868 to 1871. By Dr. GEORG SCHWEINFURTH. Translated by ELLEN E. FREWER. With an Introduction by WINWOOD READE. Illustrated by about 130 Woodcuts from Drawings made by the Author, and with Two Maps. 2 vols., 8vo, Cloth, $8 00.

Vámbéry's Central Asia.

Travels in Central Asia: being the Account of a Journey from Teheran across the Turkoman Desert, on the Eastern Shore of the Caspian, to Khiva, Bokhara, and Samarcand, performed in the Year 1863. By ARMINIUS VÁMBÉRY, Member of the Hungarian Academy of Pesth, by whom he was sent on this Scientific Mission. With Map and Woodcuts. 8vo, Cloth, $4 50; Half Calf, $6 75.

PUBLISHED BY HARPER & BROTHERS, NEW YORK.

www.ingramcontent.com/pod-product-compliance
Lightning Source LLC
Chambersburg PA
CBHW031451160426
43195CB00010BB/938